EYEWITNESS
VOLCANO &
EARTHQUAKE

Vesuv. Ash rain of the eruption
(March 1944: days 22, 23, 24, 25, 26)

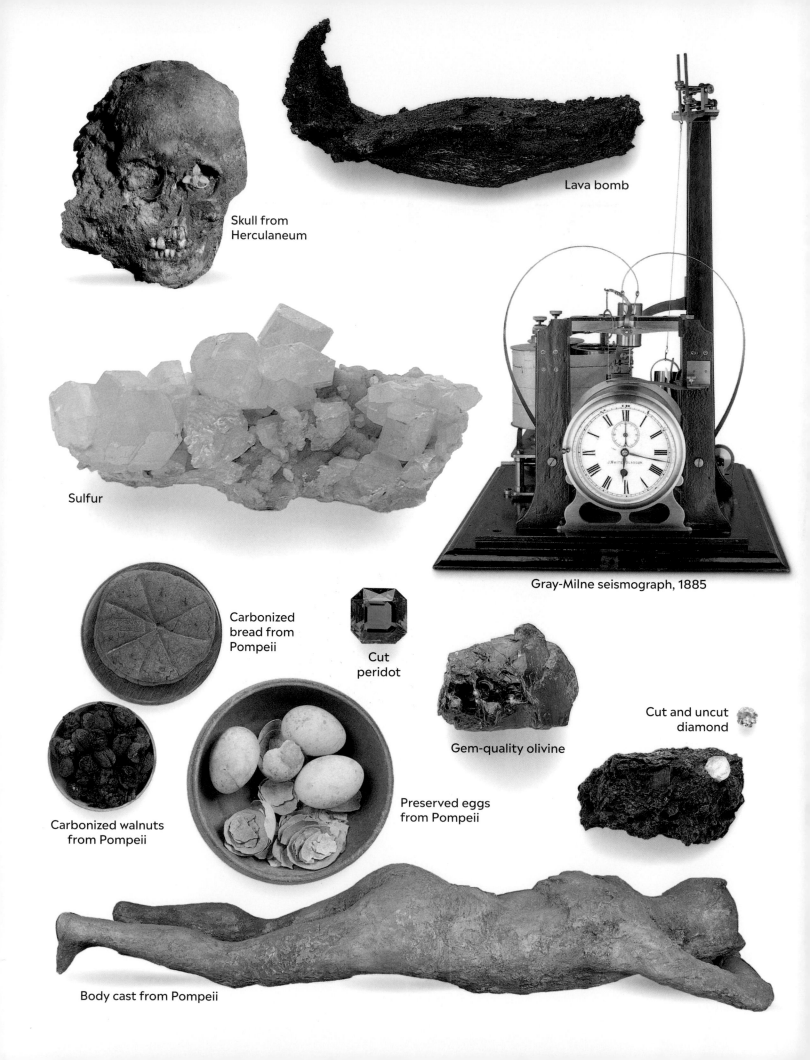

Skull from Herculaneum

Lava bomb

Sulfur

Gray-Milne seismograph, 1885

Carbonized bread from Pompeii

Cut peridot

Gem-quality olivine

Cut and uncut diamond

Carbonized walnuts from Pompeii

Preserved eggs from Pompeii

Body cast from Pompeii

Pele's hair

Voyager 1
space probe

EYEWITNESS
VOLCANO &
EARTHQUAKE

WRITTEN BY
SUSANNA VAN ROSE

**Bottle melted in
eruption of
Mount Pelée**

**Perfume bottle
melted in eruption
of Mount Pelée**

**Zhang Heng's
earthquake
detector**

Seneca, Roman philosopher who wrote about earthquake of 62 CE

REVISED EDITION

DK LONDON
Senior Editor Carron Brown
Project Editor Vicky Richards
Senior Art Editor Lynne Moulding
Art Editor Chrissy Barnard
US Senior Editor Kayla Dugger
US Executive Editor Lori Cates Hand
Managing Editor Francesca Baines
Managing Art Editor Philip Letsu
Production Editor Kavita Varma
Production Controller Sian Cheung
Senior Jackets Designer Surabhi Wadhwa-Gandhi
Jacket Design Development Manager Sophia MTT
Publisher Andrew Macintyre
Associate Publishing Director Liz Wheeler
Art Director Karen Self
Publishing Director Jonathan Metcalf

Consultant David Holmes

DK DELHI
Senior Editor Shatarupa Chaudhuri
Senior Art Editor Vikas Chauhan
Project Art Editor Heena Sharma
Editor Sai Prasanna
Picture Researcher Vishal Ghavri
Managing Editor Kingshuk Ghoshal
Managing Art Editor Govind Mittal
Senior DTP Designer Jagtar Singh
DTP Designers Pawan Kumar, Rakesh Kumar
Jacket Designer Juhi Sheth

FIRST EDITION
Project Editor Scott Steedman   **Art Editor** Christian Sévigny
Designer Yaël Freudmann
Managing Editor Helen Parker   **Managing Art Editor** Julia Harris
Production Louise Barratt
Picture Researcher Kathy Lockley
Special Photography James Stevenson
Editorial Consultants Professor John Guest and Dr Robin Adams

This Eyewitness ® Book has been conceived by
Dorling Kindersley Limited and Editions Gallimard

This American Edition, 2022
First American Edition, 1992
Published in the United States by DK Publishing
1745 Broadway, 20th Floor, New York, NY 10019

Copyright © 1992, 2002, 2008, 2014, 2022
DK, a Division of Penguin Random House LLC
22 23 24 25 26 10 9 8 7 6 5 4 3 2
003-327182-May/2022

A catalog record for this book is available from the Library of Congress.
ISBN 978-0-7440-5228-2 (Paperback)
ISBN 978-0-7440-5229-9 (ALB)

DK books are available at special discounts when purchased in bulk
for sales promotions, premiums, fund-raising, or educational use.
For details, contact: DK Publishing Special Markets,
1745 Broadway, 20th Floor, New York, NY 10019
SpecialSales@dk.com

Printed and bound in China

For the curious
www.dk.com

Fork and pocket watch damaged in eruption of Mount Pelée

Mining transit

Figure of Zhang Heng, Chinese seismologist

Lava stalagmite

Contents

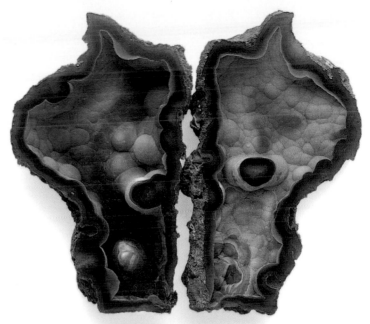

Brown agate

Wall painting

Nearly 8,000 years old, this wall painting is the earliest known picture of a volcano. It shows an eruption of the Hasan Dag volcano in Turkey.

Spitting fire

Mount Etna rises 11,122 ft (3,390 m) over the Italian island of Sicily and is one of the highest and most active volcanoes in Europe. The nearby town of Catania is occasionally showered with ash from explosions.

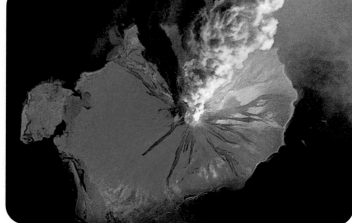

Ashy volcano

Observing ashy volcanic eruptions (pp.14–15) from the ground can be dangerous. This image of the Augustine volcano in Alaska was taken from the safety of a satellite. The ash cloud is being blasted 7 miles (11 km) high.

An unstable Earth

Volcanoes and earthquakes are nature run wild. An erupting volcano may ooze rivers of red-hot lava or spew great clouds of ash and gas into the sky. During a severe earthquake, the ground can shake so violently that entire cities are reduced to rubble. These natural disasters can be terrifying. But most eruptions and earthquakes cause little damage to people or property.

Ash treatment

Volcanic eruptions can have benefits. In Japan, being buried in warm volcanic ash is thought to be good for the health.

Perfect volcano

The graceful slopes of Mount Fujiyama in Japan are shown in this print by Katsushika Hokusai (1760–1849). This dormant (sleeping) volcano (pp.38–39) is an almost perfect cone.

Around **350 million** people in the world live within the danger range of an active volcano.

Old Faithful

Geysers spit boiling water high into the air (pp.36–37). Old Faithful, an American geyser, has erupted every hour for at least 100 years.

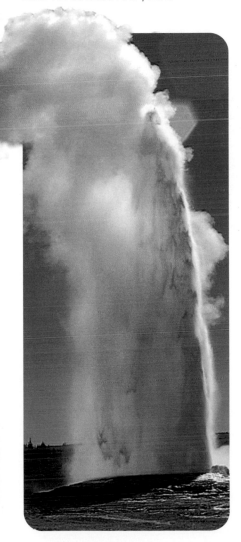

Historic earthquakes

Three major earthquakes struck Japan between 1854 and 1855. The Ansei Edo earthquake (left) occurred on November 11, 1855. The earthquake and subsequent fires resulted in 8,000–10,000 deaths.

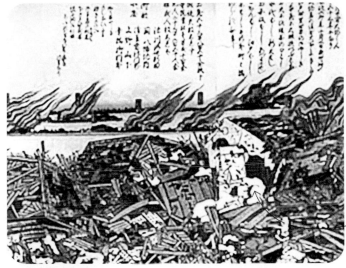

Japanese print showing the damage caused by the Ansei Edo earthquake

San Francisco, 1989

In 1906, San Francisco, California, was flattened by an enormous earthquake. Earthquakes of this size seem to rock the area every hundred years or so. A smaller quake on October 17, 1989, shook many waterfront houses off their foundations. Around 62 people died in the 15 seconds of shaking.

Hot as hell

In the Christian religion, hell is described as a fiery underworld, as shown in this 1788 painting by Irish artist James Barry.

Fire from below

Deep inside Earth, rocks melt into a thick liquid called magma (molten rock). Most of the molten rock spewed out by volcanoes comes from the top of the mantle—a layer that lies between Earth's crust and its outer core. Because magma is hotter and lighter than the surrounding rocks, it rises, melting some of the rocks it passes on the way. If it manages to find a way to the surface, the magma will erupt as lava.

Channels of fire

In this 17th-century engraving, Athanasius Kircher imagined that Earth had a fiery core that fed all the volcanoes on the surface. We now know that little of the planet's interior is liquid.

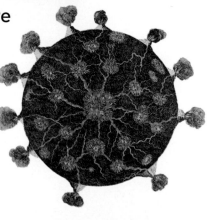

Basalt

The ocean floors that cover three-quarters of Earth's surface are made of a dark, volcanic rock called basalt.

Red-hot lava (liquid rock) shoots out of a volcano in a curtain of fire

Layers of Earth

Just like an apple, Earth is made up of layers. Its core is surrounded by a moving layer of rock called the mantle. The hard, outer layer is known as the crust.

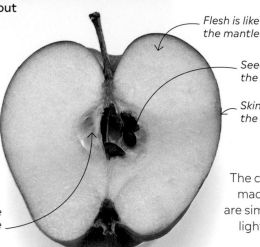

Flesh is like the mantle

Seeds are like the inner core

Skin is like the crust

Core is like the outer core

Granite

The continents are made of rocks that are similar to granite—a lighter rock than basalt.

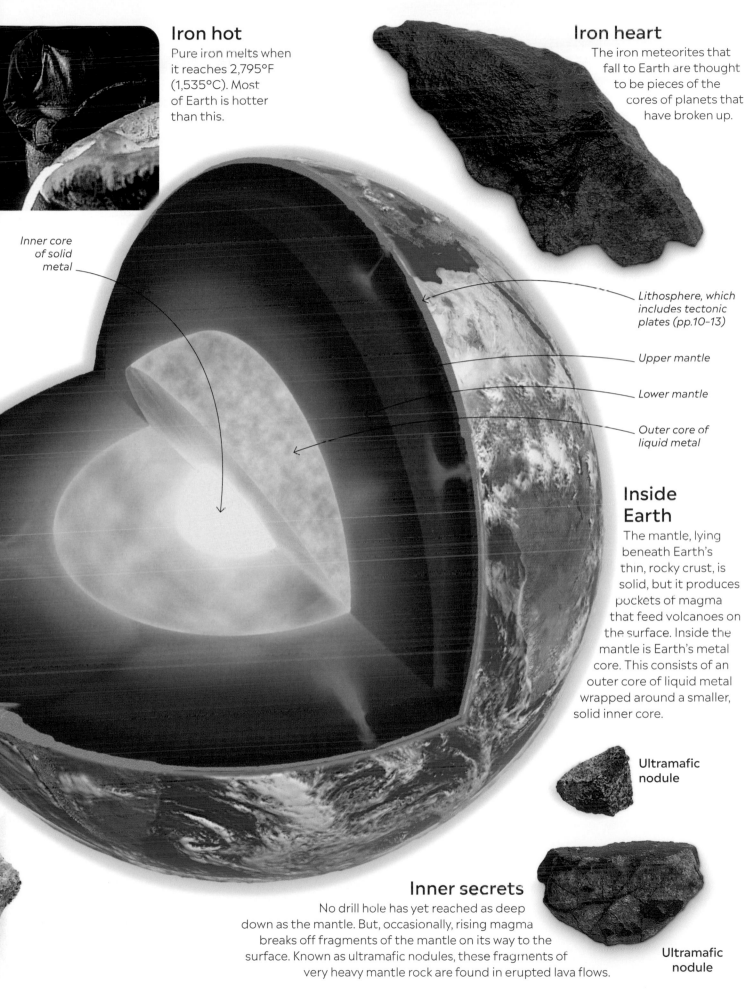

Iron hot

Pure iron melts when it reaches 2,795°F (1,535°C). Most of Earth is hotter than this.

Iron heart

The iron meteorites that fall to Earth are thought to be pieces of the cores of planets that have broken up.

Inner core of solid metal

Lithosphere, which includes tectonic plates (pp.10–13)

Upper mantle

Lower mantle

Outer core of liquid metal

Inside Earth

The mantle, lying beneath Earth's thin, rocky crust, is solid, but it produces pockets of magma that feed volcanoes on the surface. Inside the mantle is Earth's metal core. This consists of an outer core of liquid metal wrapped around a smaller, solid inner core.

Ultramafic nodule

Inner secrets

No drill hole has yet reached as deep down as the mantle. But, occasionally, rising magma breaks off fragments of the mantle on its way to the surface. Known as ultramafic nodules, these fragments of very heavy mantle rock are found in erupted lava flows.

Ultramafic nodule

Carrying the weight of the world

In Roman mythology, the god Atlas held the sky on his shoulders. In this statue, he carries the entire globe.

Tectonic plates

Volcanoes and earthquakes are more common in some parts of the world than others. In the 1960s, the secrets of the deep ocean floor began to be revealed. Scientists discovered that Earth's crust is made up of huge slabs of rock that fit together like odd-shaped paving stones. Called tectonic plates, these chunks of rock move constantly across the surface of the planet at a rate of a few centimeters a year. Most volcanoes and earthquakes occur at plate boundaries where the tectonic plates collide, rub together, or move apart.

Pacific Ring of Fire

Ring of Fire

The "Ring of Fire" is an area in the Pacific Ocean where most of the world's volcanic and earthquake activity occurs. On this map, the red triangles are volcanoes and the yellow dots are locations where earthquakes occur frequently.

Most volcanoes form along the boundaries of the tectonic plates (red lines).

👁 EYEWITNESS

Continental drifter

German scientist Alfred Wegener (1880–1930) first used the term "continental drift." He noticed that the coastlines of South America and Africa fit together, concluding that they had once been part of a bigger single continent but later drifted apart. Largely ignored at first, his ideas were only accepted when spreading ridges (pp.24–25) were discovered 40 years later.

Lessons of history

This plaster cast shows a man killed in the eruption of Mount Vesuvius, which devastated the Roman towns of Pompeii and Herculaneum in 79 CE (pp.26–31).

Living on the Ring of Fire

Volcanoes and earthquakes are frequent events in Japan. This huge quake in 1925 damaged the ancient city of Kyoto.

Alaska and the Aleutian Islands have many volcanoes and earthquakes.

Iceland sits on top of the Mid-Atlantic spreading ridge (pp.24–25).

Like Japan, Kamchatka is part of the Pacific Ring of Fire.

These lines show where two or more plates meet.

The Mid-Atlantic Ridge is part of the largest mountain range in the world.

The island of Réunion was formed by a hot spot (pp.22–23) that was under India 30 million years ago.

Antarctica is surrounded by new ocean made by spreading ridges (pp.24–25).

Indonesia, home to over 125 active volcanoes, is at the boundary of two plates.

Mount Erebus, an active volcano in Antarctica

Drifting plates

This globe has been colored to highlight the tectonic plates. It is the plates, and not the continents, that are on the move.

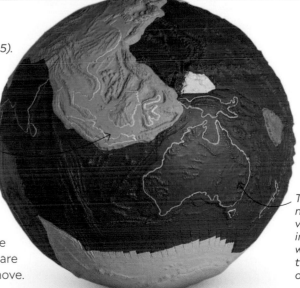

There are no active volcanoes in Australia, which sits in the middle of a plate.

Fire-land

Iceland is made almost entirely of volcanic rocks like those found on the deep ocean floor. It has gradually built up above sea level through intense and prolonged eruptions.

Moving plates

Most volcanoes are found at plate boundaries, where melting rock forms columns of magma that erupt at the surface. When two plates move apart, a chain of gentle volcanoes, known as a spreading ridge, is formed. Where plates collide, one is forced beneath the other, forming a subduction zone. The sinking plate partly melts and the hot, liquid magma rises. A third kind of volcano erupts above a hot spot, a place where rising magma burns through Earth's crust.

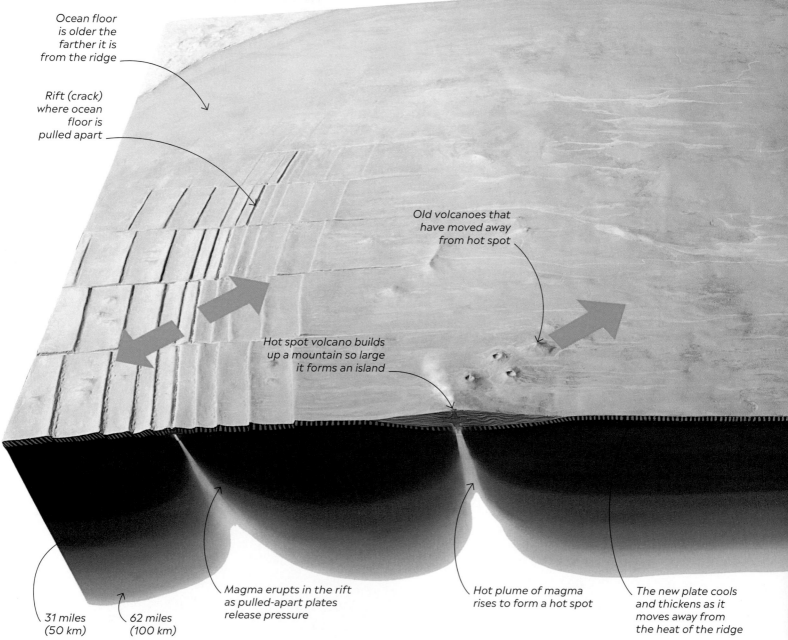

Ocean floor is older the farther it is from the ridge

Rift (crack) where ocean floor is pulled apart

Old volcanoes that have moved away from hot spot

Hot spot volcano builds up a mountain so large it forms an island

31 miles (50 km)

62 miles (100 km)

Magma erupts in the rift as pulled-apart plates release pressure

Hot plume of magma rises to form a hot spot

The new plate cools and thickens as it moves away from the heat of the ridge

Spreading ridges

New ocean floor is made where plates are pulled apart (pp.24–25), creating a rift (crack in Earth's crust). Here, magma erupts as lava, creating new rock. All the ocean floor has been made this way in the last 200 million years.

Hot spots

Hot spots (pp.22–23) are areas in the middle of a tectonic plate where columns of magma from the mantle rise to the surface and punch a hole in the plate, forming a volcano.

Volcano chain

Guatemala in Central America is home to a chain of volcanoes, many still active. They sit on top of a subduction zone, formed as the Cocos Plate sinks beneath the larger North American Plate.

America's fault

The San Andreas Fault is probably the most famous plate boundary in the world. The plates, which constantly slide against each other, move about 1–1½ in (3–5 cm) a year.

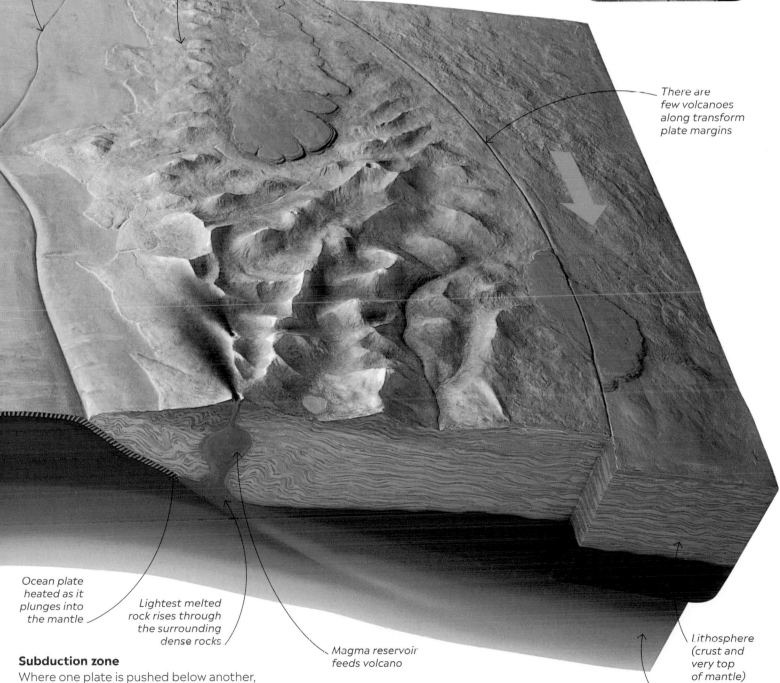

Deep ocean trench is formed where the ocean floor descends in a subduction zone

Continental boundary lifted above subduction zone

There are few volcanoes along transform plate margins

Ocean plate heated as it plunges into the mantle

Lightest melted rock rises through the surrounding dense rocks

Magma reservoir feeds volcano

Lithosphere (crust and very top of mantle)

Asthenosphere (soft, upper part of mantle)

Subduction zone

Where one plate is pushed below another, it sinks into the mantle, partly melting some rocks to form magma. This magma erupts at the surface through volcanoes.

Transform plate margin

Where two plates meet at an odd angle, a boundary called a transform plate margin is formed.

Mount St. Helens

Summit altitude of 9,677 ft (2,950 m) before eruption

Slumbering giant
Before the eruption, Mount St. Helens had a beautiful, snow-capped peak.

When Mount St. Helens, a volcano in the Cascade range in the northwestern US, blew its top on May 18, 1980, it had been quiet for 123 years. The massive explosion was heard in Vancouver, Canada, 200 miles (320 km) away. The blast tore off most of the north side of the volcano, leaving a gaping hole. Pyroclastic flows of hot ash and gas (p.16) rushed down the slopes at terrifying speeds. The explosion continued for nine hours, sending millions of tons of ash 14 miles (22 km) up into the atmosphere. Vast areas of forest were flattened and 57 people were killed.

38 seconds after the first explosion
After two months of small explosions, the north slope of Mount St. Helens suddenly shivered and seemed to turn to liquid. This picture, taken 38 seconds into the explosion, shows the avalanche roaring down the north face and a cloud of ash and gas blasting skyward.

Moving wall of ash
As the ash cloud blasted out, it became lighter than air and began to rise. Gary Rosenquist took this picture before he ran for his car. "The turbulent cloud loomed behind us as we sped down Road 99," he wrote later. "Mudballs flattened against the windshield. Minutes later, it was completely dark."

The eruption of
Mount St. Helens
destroyed
230 sq miles
(600 sq km)
of forests.

FEEDING THE FURY

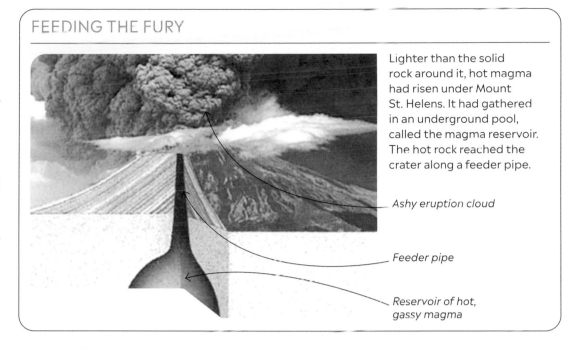

Lighter than the solid rock around it, hot magma had risen under Mount St. Helens. It had gathered in an underground pool, called the magma reservoir. The hot rock reached the crater along a feeder pipe.

Ashy eruption cloud

Feeder pipe

Reservoir of hot, gassy magma

Four seconds later ...

... the avalanche of old rock had been overtaken by the darker, growing cloud of ash, which contained newly erupted material. Gary Rosenquist, who took these pictures from 11 miles (18 km) away, said later that "the sight ... was so overwhelming that I became dizzy and had to turn away to keep my balance."

Eleven seconds later ...

... the avalanche of old rock had been completely overtaken by the faster blast of ash. On the right, huge chunks of rock could be seen as they were catapulted out of the cloud.

Last gasp

In the months after the eruption, thick, sticky lava was squeezed from the magma reservoir like toothpaste from a tube. It formed a bulging dome, which reached a height of 853 ft (260 m) in 1986. The dome later crumbled into lava fragments.

Flattened forests

Mature forests of trees up to 164 ft (50 m) tall were flattened by the blast of the eruption.

Ash and **dust**

Lapilli, bite-sized fragments of frothy lava

Ash, smaller pyroclastic fragments

Explosive volcanoes pour clouds of ash into the sky. The ash is formed from volcanic rock that has been blown into billions of tiny pieces. These rock fragments, known as pyroclastics, range from huge lava blocks (p.18) to fine, powdery dust (pp.34–35). Between these two extremes are lapilli (Latin for "little stones") and ash. Sometimes the ash clouds collapse under their own weight, forming pyroclastic flows or surges. Unlike lava flows, pyroclastic flows can be extremely dangerous.

Dust, the smallest and lightest lava fragments

Constructing a cone

Mountains are built up as pyroclastic fragments settle in layers on a volcano's slopes. Gassy fire-fountain eruptions build cinder cones of bombs and ash.

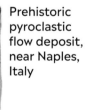

Prehistoric pyroclastic flow deposit, near Naples, Italy

Volcano biography

Frozen in a volcano's slopes is a record of its past eruptions. The rock layers can be dated and their textures analyzed. The ash layers in this rock were erupted by an English volcano about 500 million years ago.

Glowing avalanches

If the erupted mixture of hot rocks and gas is heavier than air, it may flow downhill at more than 60 mph (100 kph). Such a pyroclastic flow may flatten everything in its path. Equally destructive are pyroclastic surges—flows that contain more hot gas than ash.

Fine-grained ash

Pumice bomb

Detail of Neapolitan pyroclastic flow deposit

Lithic (old lava) fragment

Their fields buried in ash, farmers take their buffaloes and head for greener pastures.

Buried crops

A thin fall of ash fertilizes the soil (pp.40–41), but too much destroys crops. Whole harvests were lost in the heavy ash falls that followed the eruptions of Mount Pinatubo.

Night of the ash cloud

After lying dormant for 600 years, Mount Pinatubo in the Philippines began erupting in June 1991. Huge clouds of ash were thrown into the air, blocking out the sunlight for days. Over 330 ft (100 m) of ash lay on the upper slopes of the volcano. Torrential rains followed, causing mud flows that swept away roads, bridges, and several villages (p.56). At least 400 people were killed and another 400,000 were left homeless.

👁 EYEWITNESS

Studying Pinatubo

A geologist from the Philippine Institute of Volcanology and Seismology, Bella Tubianosa has studied Mount Pinatubo along with other researchers in order to map and predict its blasts. Here, she is examining deposits and taking temperatures of the pyroclastic flow days after the eruption in 1991.

Fiery rocks

Volcanoes erupt red-hot lava. Sometimes the lava oozes gently from a hole in the ground. At other times, it is hurled into the air in spectacular fire fountains. When it lands, the lava flows down in rivers of hot rock that can cover the countryside. If the lava is less fluid, explosions may occur as volcanic gas escapes from the hot rock. These explosions throw out chunks of flying lava, known as bombs and blocks.

Reheated lava

Some of the gas dissolved in lava is lost when it cools. This piece of lava frothed up when it was reheated, showing that it still contained a lot of its original gas.

Bomb thrown out by Mount Etna on the island of Sicily in Italy (pp.6–7)

Dense, round bomb

Bombs and blocks

Bombs and blocks can be as big as houses or as small as tennis balls. Bombs are usually more rounded, while blocks are more dense and angular. Their shapes depend upon how fluid or gassy the lava was during the eruption.

Small, explosive eruption photographed on Mount Etna in 2013

Twisted tail

The odd twists and tails of many bombs are formed as they spin through the air.

Hawaiian aa
Glowing red at night, the intense heat of an aa flow shows through the surface crust of cooling lava. Lava flows take a long time to cool. As they harden, the flows grow thicker and slow down.

Aa and pahoehoe flows

Lava flows pose little danger to people, as they rarely travel faster than a few miles an hour. The two kinds of flows get their names from Hawaiian words. Aa (pronounced *ah-ah*) flows are covered in sharp, angular chunks of lava known as scoria. Pahoehoe (*pa-hoy-hoy*) flows grow a smooth skin soon after they leave the vent.

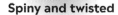

Hardened chunk of ropy pahoehoe lava

Pahoehoe flows
Pahoehoe is more fluid than aa and contains more gas. As its surface cools, the flow grows a thin skin. The hot lava on the inside makes the skin wrinkle, so its surface looks like the coils of a rope. The crust may grow so thick that people can walk across it while red-hot lava flows in a tunnel below (p.23).

Spiny and twisted
This chunk of scoria from the surface of an aa flow was twisted as it was carried along.

Driblets of remelted lava from the roof of a pahoehoe tunnel

Black sand from the volcanic island of Santorini, Greece

Pahoehoe toe
This picture shows red-hot pahoehoe bulging through a crack in its own skin. New skin is forming over the bulge. A pahoehoe flow creeps forward with thousands of little breakouts like this one.

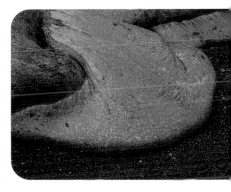

Fire and water
Volcanic islands like Hawaii are usually fringed by black beaches. The sand is formed when hot lava hits the sea and is shattered into tiny particles. It is black because the lava is rich in dark minerals.

Lava from Kilauea volcano in Hawaii flowing into the Pacific Ocean

Gas and **lightning**

Volcanic gases are extremely dangerous. In August 1986, an explosion in Lake Nyos in Cameroon, Africa, released a cloud of volcanic gases. The poisonous fumes killed 1,700 people living in villages nearby. The main killer was carbon dioxide, which has no odor and is very hard to detect. Other volcanic gases, on the other hand, are extremely smelly; hydrogen sulfide, for example, smells like rotten eggs, and the acid gases hydrogen chloride and sulfur dioxide sting the eyes and throat. They also eat through clothes, leaving holes with bleached haloes around them.

Steam-assisted eruption

When the new island of Surtsey was formed off Iceland in 1963 (p.41), seawater poured into the volcano's vent and hit the hot magma, producing spectacular explosions and huge clouds of steam.

Raising a stink

Nearly 40 years after the last eruption of Kawah Idjen in Java, Indonesia, sulfur and other gases are still escaping into the volcano's crater.

Captain Haddock and friends flee from a volcano's gases in the Tintin adventure *Flight 714*

Volcanologist studying Hawaiian lava flows behind the safety of a gas mask

Gas mask

Made to protect the wearer against low concentrations of acid gases, this gas mask also keeps out all but the finest volcanic dust.

Floating rock

The volcanic rock pumice is light because it is full of bubbles of gas. Some pumice is light enough to float on water.

Vesuvius

Lord Hamilton, British ambassador to Naples, saw lightning flashes as he watched the 1779 eruption of Vesuvius (p.31).

Floating on an acid lake

Volcanologists sample volcanic gases from an acid lake in the crater of Kawah Idjen. The gases rising from the volcano are dissolved in the lake water that fills much of the crater. Such acid lakes are very hostile to life and would burn a swimmer's skin in minutes.

Lightning flash

Immense flashes of lightning are often seen during eruptions. They are caused by a build-up of static electricity produced when tiny fragments of lava in an ash cloud rub against each other. This picture shows lightning bolts at the volcano Eyjafjallajökull in Iceland on April 18, 2010.

Mauna Loa erupts

Two of the world's biggest volcanoes, Mauna Loa and Kilauea, are on the volcanic island of Hawaii. Here, fire fountains erupting from Mauna Loa have created black cinder cones made of ash and bombs (p.16).

Hot spots

The largest volcanoes on Earth are found above hot spots—areas deep within Earth's mantle that produce huge volumes of magma. When the hot magma rises, it burns through Earth's crust, creating a volcano (pp.12–13). Many volcanic islands, such as Iceland and Hawaii, are located above hot spots. The Hawaiian island chain is part of a huge undersea mountain range that formed over millions of years as the hot spot erupted great volumes of lava onto the moving plate above it.

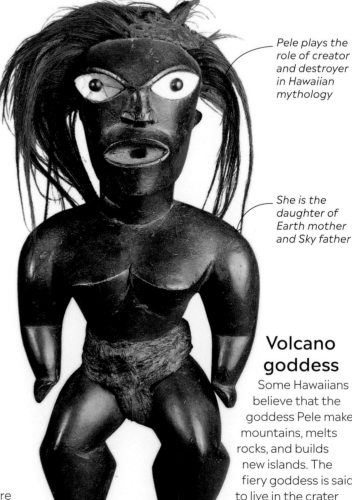

Pele plays the role of creator and destroyer in Hawaiian mythology

She is the daughter of Earth mother and Sky father

A STRING OF ISLANDS

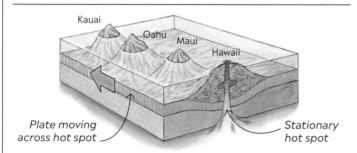

Kauai
Oahu
Maui
Hawaii

Plate moving across hot spot

Stationary hot spot

The Pacific Plate is moving over the stationary Hawaiian hot spot, under the south end of the island. In addition to Mauna Loa and Kilauea, a third volcano, Loihi, is growing below the sea to the south. The north end of Hawaii is made up of older, extinct volcanoes.

Volcano goddess

Some Hawaiians believe that the goddess Pele makes mountains, melts rocks, and builds new islands. The fiery goddess is said to live in the crater Halema'uma'u, at the summit of Kilauea.

Pele's hair

The hot, fluid lava of a Hawaiian fire fountain may be blown into fine, glassy strands. These are known as Pele's hair.

Stalagmites grow upward from the floor

Lava stalagmite made of drips in a pahoehoe tube

◉ EYEWITNESS

Hot spotter

Canadian geophysicist John Tuzo-Wilson (1908–1993) first suggested that plates move over fixed "hot spots" in the mantle, forming volcanic island chains. He introduced the term "transform faults"—boundaries where two plates slide past each other.

Lava has solidified around this tree, leaving a tree mold

Road buried by lava during eruption of Kilauea

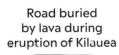

Up in flames

Lava in tubes remains hot and fluid, so it can travel many miles, engulfing land and villages on the way.

Lava tube

The skin of a pahoehoe flow (p.19) may crust over into a roof thick enough to walk on. Only a yard or so below, hot lava continues to run in a tunnel or "tube." Lava dripping off the underside of the roof creates strange formations called lava stalagmites (far left) and stalactites.

Moving hot spot

This volcano is Piton de la Fournaise on the island of Réunion in the Indian Ocean (p.11). The island is the tip of a huge volcano that rises 4 miles (7 km) above the ocean floor. The hot spot has moved 2,500 miles (4,000 km) in the last 30 million years.

Red Sea

A spreading ridge runs through the Red Sea. For the last 20 million years, it has been making a new ocean floor, as Arabia moves away from Africa.

Icelandic eruptions give a glimpse of how spreading ridges make new oceanic plates. The eruptions tend to be from long cracks rather than central craters.

Submersible *Alvin*, taking photos of ridges

Ocean **floor**

New ocean floor is constantly being made by volcanic eruptions beneath the waters. Spreading ridges form where two plates pull apart, creating a rift (crack) in the ocean floor. Here, the lava erupts gently, forming rounded shapes known as pillow lava. This new rock fills in the widening rift as the plates pull farther apart. In this way, the oceans grow just a little wider—a centimeter or so—a year. In places, the rifts are bubbling with hot springs, known as black smokers, that are home to a variety of strange lifeforms.

Undersea volcano

This undersea volcano erupted off the coast of Tonga on March 18, 2009. It spewed plumes of ash, steam, and smoke up to 328 ft (100 m) into the air.

New seafloor

Seafloor spreading is a geological process that occurs at mid-ocean ridges, where tectonic plates split from each other. As the plates diverge, the crust cracks and hot magma fills the fractures. The magma cools to form igneous rock, creating new seafloor.

Mid-ocean ridge

Molten rock

Volcanic island

Deep sea trench

Part of undersea volcano showing above water

Black smokers

These strange chimneylike structures are found along spreading ridges on the ocean floor. The black, acidic water that gushes up from these hot springs is rich in valuable metal minerals produced by the new ocean plate that is formed at the ridges.

MODEL OF BLACK SMOKER

Cold water seeps down through cracks in the ocean floor, gets heated, and rises up.

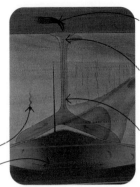

Plume of black metal minerals

Black smoker chimney

Feeder channel or pipe

Cold sea water seeping through hot rock

Magma reservoir

Chimney pipes
When the rising minerals meet the chilled ocean water, they cool and harden to form the chimney pipes that surround the black smokers. These grow steadily, collapsing only when they get too tall.

Black smoker hydrothermal vent in the Pacific Ocean

Sulfur-eating tube worms

Lava feeder channels
Two ancient lava feeder channels can be seen in the rock above.

Manganese nodules
The ocean floor is carpeted with black lumps that are rich in manganese and other metals.

Gabbro, a coarsely crystalline rock from an old seafloor magma reservoir in Cyprus

Rounded, pillow-shaped underwater lava

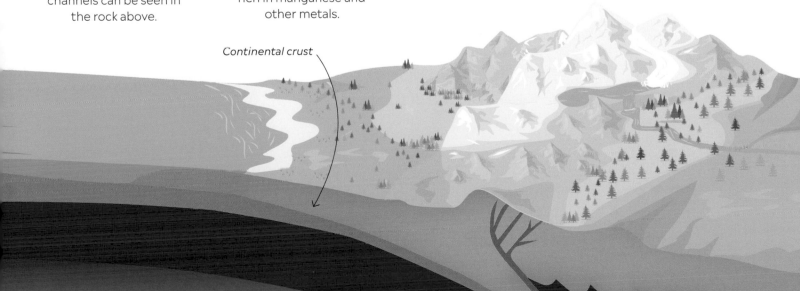

Continental crust

Mount Vesuvius

Perhaps the most famous eruption of all time was that of Mount Vesuvius near Naples, Italy. When the long-dormant volcano erupted in 79 CE, the residents of the Roman towns of Pompeii and Herculaneum were caught unaware. Hot ash and stones rained down on Pompeii for hours until it was buried several yards deep. Many trying to flee were overwhelmed by a sudden blast of ash and gas (a pyroclastic surge, p.16). The buried towns were virtually forgotten until excavations began in the 18th century. These digs have since unearthed priceless treasures.

Fresh walnuts

Bowl of carbonized walnuts

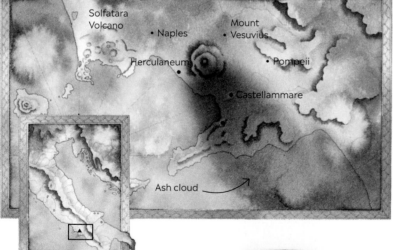

Solfatara Volcano

• Naples

Mount • Vesuvius

Herculaneum

• Pompeii

• Castellammare

Ash cloud

Charcoal

Objects that contain carbon, like wood or food, usually burn when heated. But when there is not enough oxygen for them to burn in the normal way, they turn to charcoal instead. This process, called carbonization, left many foodstuffs perfectly preserved in the ash.

Guard dog mosaics were common at Pompeii home entrances.

Mills could be driven by donkeys

Blowing in the wind

Herculaneum was hardly touched by the falling ash that rained on Pompeii. But the pyroclastic flows and surges (p.16) that followed affected both towns.

Flour mill made of lava, a tough rock also used to pave streets

Beware of dog

This floor mosaic from a Pompeii entrance hall was designed to warn off intruders.

Pompeii destroyed

The Italian city of Pompeii was destroyed when Mount Vesuvius erupted in 79 CE and its buildings were buried under layers of volcanic ash and rock. The ruins were discovered in 1748 and were gradually excavated.

Mount Vesuvius

Ruins of Pompeii found after excavation, as they stand today

Burnt to a toast

This carbonized loaf of bread was one of several found in the brick oven of a bakery. The baker's stamp can still be seen nearly 2,000 years after the day the bread was baked.

Baker's stamp

Broken egg shells

Bowl of preserved eggs

Bowl of carbonized figs

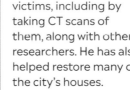

Fresh figs, still grown on the slopes of Vesuvius

EYEWITNESS

Studying Pompeii

Director of the laboratory at Pompeii Archaeological Site, Stefano Vanacore studies the ash-covered remains of Pompeii's victims, including by taking CT scans of them, along with other researchers. He has also helped restore many of the city's houses.

Buried in ashes

More than 2,000 people died in Pompeii during the eruption. As the fleeing Pompeiians fell, the rain of ash and pumice set around their bodies like wet cement. Over time, the soft body parts decayed and the ash and pumice turned to rock. The shapes of the bodies were left as hollows in the rock, with only the hard bones remaining. In 1860, the Italian king appointed Giuseppe Fiorelli as director of the excavations.

Health warning

This skeleton mosaic found near Pompeii is a "memento mori," a reminder of death.

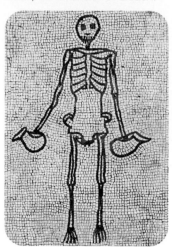

Floor mosaic of a skeleton holding wine jugs

Last day of Pompeii
This fanciful painting of the destruction of Pompeii by 19th-century Russian artist Karl Briullov shows houses catching fire.

Killed on duty
The American writer Mark Twain was most impressed by the remains of a soldier in Pompeii who had stayed at his post during the eruption.

MAKING A CAST

Fiorelli invented a method for removing the skeletons from the hollows and filling the space with wet plaster of Paris. After the plaster hardened, a replica of the bodies could be dug out of the rock.

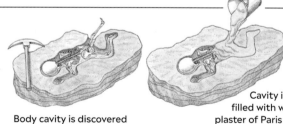

Body cavity is discovered

Cavity is filled with wet plaster of Paris

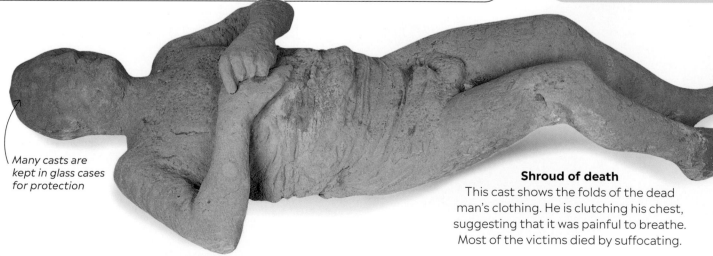

Many casts are kept in glass cases for protection

Shroud of death
This cast shows the folds of the dead man's clothing. He is clutching his chest, suggesting that it was painful to breathe. Most of the victims died by suffocating.

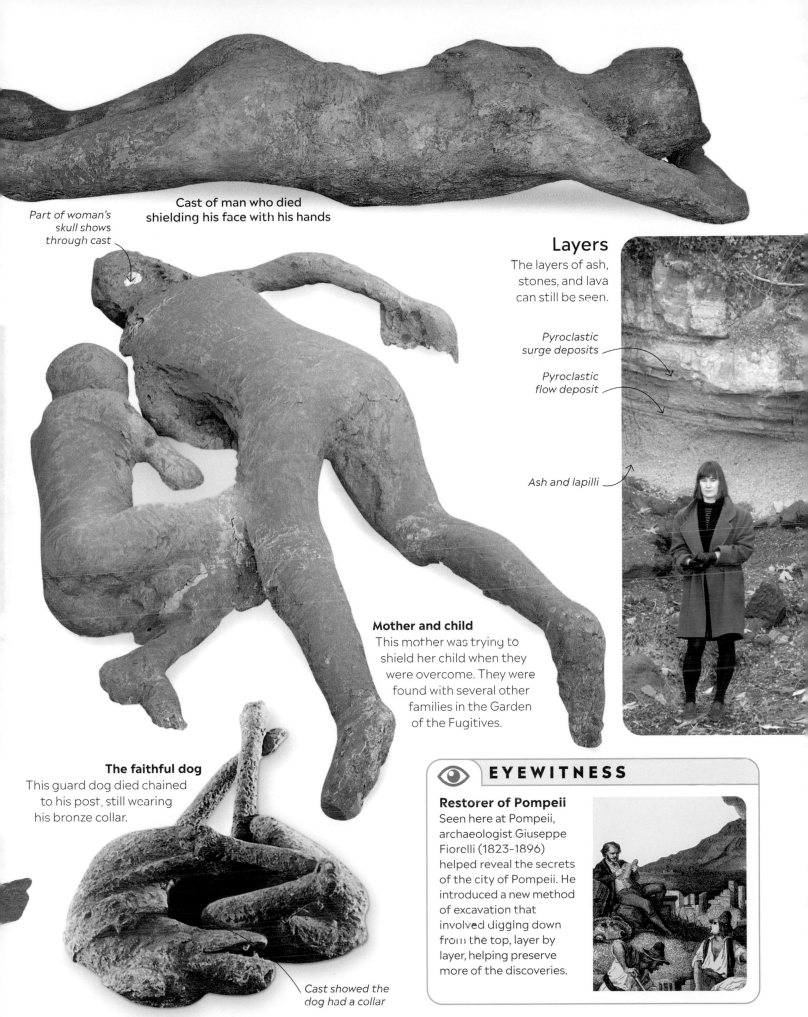

Cast of man who died shielding his face with his hands

Part of woman's skull shows through cast

Layers
The layers of ash, stones, and lava can still be seen.

Pyroclastic surge deposits

Pyroclastic flow deposit

Ash and lapilli

Mother and child
This mother was trying to shield her child when they were overcome. They were found with several other families in the Garden of the Fugitives.

The faithful dog
This guard dog died chained to his post, still wearing his bronze collar.

Cast showed the dog had a collar

Herculaneum

When Vesuvius erupted in 79 CE, the ash cloud that engulfed Pompeii missed Herculaneum (p.26). Less than 1 in (3 cm) of debris had fallen on the town when it was blasted by a great surge of hot ash and gas. Early excavations uncovered very few bodies, which was puzzling. But in the 1980s, several hundred skeletons were found huddled together beneath huge brick arches that once stood on the shoreline.

Walking in the ruins
The excavations of the Roman town have created a deep hole that is surrounded by the modern city of Herculaneum (p.60). This street is laid with lava paving stones.

Neptune and Amphitrite
This mosaic of two Roman gods was unearthed at a merchant's house in Herculaneum.

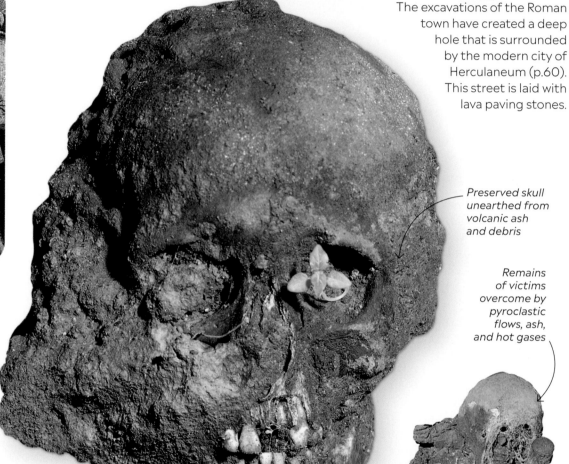

Preserved skull unearthed from volcanic ash and debris

Remains of victims overcome by pyroclastic flows, ash, and hot gases

Roman skeletons
Unlike the bones in Pompeii, the skeletons from Herculaneum have no surrounding body shape. This is because they lay in waterlogged ground and the wet ash packed tightly around the bones.

A tomb of hot rock
Herculaneum was hit by six pyroclastic surges (pp.16–17) followed by thick flows of hot ash, pumice, and rock. These flows buried the town in 66 ft (20 m) of volcanic debris.

1631 eruption

Hamilton's view
Lord Hamilton (p.21) included this view of the 1779 eruption in his book *The Campi Phlegraei*. The artist is Pietro Fabris (p.39).

The most visited volcano

The Romans who lived in the shadow of Vesuvius were scarcely aware that it was a volcano. The mountain had erupted 800 years earlier, but it had been calm since. The biggest recent eruption, in 1631, produced pyroclastic surges and flows. In the 18th century, travelers flocked to Naples to visit the angry mountain. Even today, tourists climb to the summit and pay to look into the steaming crater.

On the tourist map
This cartoon shows English tourists at Vesuvius in 1890. A guidebook of 1883 advises sightseers to wear their worst clothes because boots could be ruined by the sharp lava and dresses stained by the sulfur.

Photograph of tourists watching the 1933 eruption

Vesuv. Ash rain of the eruption (March 1944: days 22. 23. 24. 25. 26)

Souvenir of Vesuvius
Centuries ago, souvenirs from Naples included Roman artifacts stolen from the excavations. These days, security is tighter, and boxes of lava and ash are more common souvenirs.

Textbook eruption
This 1767 engraving, which probably shows the 1760 eruption, was published in an 18th-century textbook.

German etching of 1885 eruption showing fires started by lava flows

St. Pierre

One of the worst volcanic disasters of the 20th century happened on the Caribbean island of Martinique. On May 8, 1902, Mount Pelée—the volcano that towered over the city of St. Pierre—erupted just before 8 A.M. The mountain sent a cloud of glowing gas down upon the port, and all its inhabitants were engulfed. Within minutes, St. Pierre was charred beyond recognition. A few sailors survived on their ships, but all except two of the city's 29,000 residents were killed.

Melted medicine bottle

Carbonized spaghetti

Carbonized prune

Ash fragment

Fine volcanic ash melted into glaze

Melted glass

Melted wine bottle

Discovered in the 1950s, these partly melted objects give a glimpse of everyday life in the small French colony at the beginning of the 20th century. Some objects are either so melted or so unfamiliar that it is hard to guess what they are.

Melted metal fork (rust occurred after eruption)

Stopped clock

This pocket watch was melted to a standstill at 8:15 A.M.

Ruined city

The walls of some buildings were all that was left standing in St. Pierre. Many died in the cathedral, where mass had just begun.

Mount Pelée

Present-day view of St. Pierre

Carbonized coffee beans

Charred mug

EYEWITNESS

Silver lining
One of the two survivors in St. Pierre was 25-year-old Auguste Ciparis, a condemned prisoner. He survived because his cell had thick walls and a tiny window. He was later pardoned and became part of a circus act.

BARNUM & BAILEY
GREATEST SHOW ON EARTH
ROGER SYLBARIS
LIVING OBJECT THAT SURVIVED IN THE "SILENT CITY OF DEATH" WHERE 40000 HUMAN BEINGS ROASTED BURNED OR BURIED BEFORE BELCHING BLAST OF MONT PELÉE'S TERRIBLE VOLCANIC ERUPTION

Eternal figure
The wooden cross was burned off this crucifix, leaving just the figure of Jesus.

Heap of fused iron nails

Top of charred human femur (thigh bone)

Petrified
Some objects containing carbon were scorched or burned completely. Others were carbonized (pp.26-27).

Melted metal spoon

Fused coins

Protecting angel?
This angel figurine made of metal is just about recognizable.

Squashed candlestick

Broken statuette

Heap of glass melted beyond recognition

EYEWITNESS

Alfred Lacroix (1863-1948)
French volcanologist Alfred Lacroix arrived in St. Pierre on June 23. In his report on Mount Pelée, he described strange "glowing clouds." Nowadays, these are known as pyroclastic flows or surges (p.16).

Affecting
global climate

A big, ashy volcanic eruption has a dramatic effect on both the global climate and local weather. Dark days, severe winds, and heavy rain may plague the local area for months. If the gas and dust are thrown high into the atmosphere, they can spread around the world, affecting the climate of the whole planet. The volcanic material filters out some sunlight, reducing temperatures down below. In the longer term, volcanic particles may cause global cooling, mass extinctions, or even ice ages.

Little Ice Age
Two major eruptions in Iceland and Japan in 1783 led to several icy winters in Europe and America.

Dinosaurs
It is likely that the dinosaurs died out due to climate change caused by a major asteroid impact and huge volcanic eruptions that occurred around 66 million years ago.

Early Earth
About 4 billion years ago, planet Earth had no atmosphere and its surface was covered with erupting volcanoes. All the water in the oceans and many of the gases that make up the atmosphere have been produced by volcanic eruptions.

Earth covered with volcanoes

Tyrannosaurus rex

Volcanic sunset
Eruptions can cause unusually red sunsets. This sunset was caused by dust from the 1980 eruption of Mount St. Helens (pp.14–15).

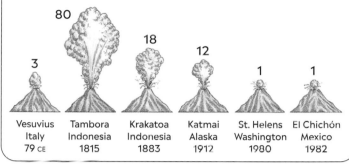

3	80	18	12	1	1
Vesuvius Italy 79 CE	Tambora Indonesia 1815	Krakatoa Indonesia 1883	Katmai Alaska 1912	St. Helens Washington 1980	El Chichón Mexico 1982

Floating around the globe

The June 1991 eruptions of Mount Pinatubo in the Philippines (above and p.17) spewed ash and gas into the stratosphere. Satellite images (above) showed that by July 25, the particles had spread around the world.

Krakatoa

In 1883, the Indonesian island of Krakatoa was blown to pieces in a massive eruption. The explosion was heard 2,485 miles (4,000 km) away in Australia. Floating islands of pumice drifted across the Indian Ocean for months afterward. This piece was washed up on a beach in Madagascar, 4,350 miles (7,000 km) away.

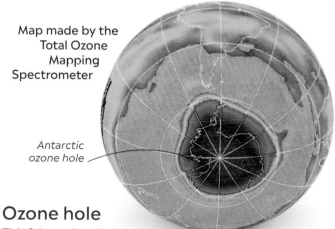

Map made by the Total Ozone Mapping Spectrometer

Antarctic ozone hole

Ozone hole

This false-colored satellite image shows the hole in the ozone layer over the Antarctic. Sulfur particles thrown up by Pinatubo may cause further damage to this protective layer. This could affect world temperatures.

Airport display panels show all flights canceled

Ash across the sky

In 2010, much of European airspace was shut for days when ash from the Eyjafjallajökull eruption spread fast with the winds.

In hot water

In volcanic areas, heat from the rocks also heats the water in the ground. During long dormant (inactive) periods, the hot water may shoot to the surface in steam vents, geysers, hot springs, and pools of bubbling mud. These hydrothermal (hot water) features can be put to good use. Steam can be used to generate electricity and hot groundwater can help heat homes and greenhouses.

Measuring Earth's heat

An instrument called a thermocouple is being used to measure the heat of a steam vent, or fumarole, in the Solfatara crater. Temperatures here can reach 284°F (140°C). Changes in the heat and gas can give clues to future volcanic eruptions.

Crystals of sulfur

The sulfur in volcanic gas cools and forms crystals. These huge, yellow crystals are from Sicily, where sulfur has been mined for centuries. Sulfur has many uses, particularly in manufacturing. It is added to rubber to make it more durable in a process called vulcanization—named after the Roman fire god Vulcan.

Healing powers

Water that has been superheated by lava flows is used to create a beautiful pool at the Blue Lagoon spa in Iceland. Tourists from all around the world come to bathe in its mineral-rich waters, thought to benefit the skin.

Hot water power

About 40 percent of Iceland's electricity comes from hydrothermal power stations. Countries such as Japan and the US are also developing hydrothermal power programs.

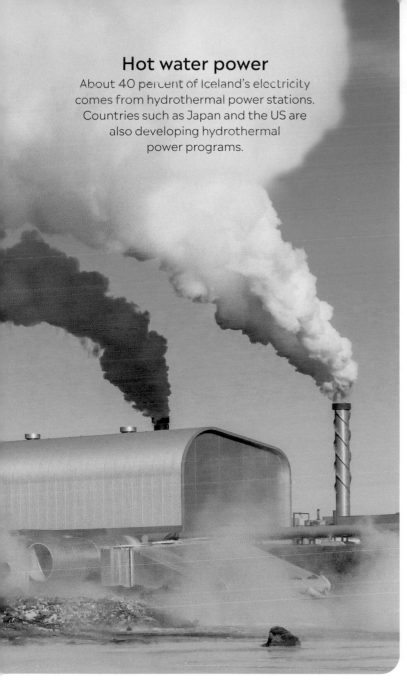

Souvenir plate showing Old Faithful Geyser, US (p.7)

Bubbling mud

Some fumaroles bubble up through a mud bath of their own making. The acid sulfur gases eat into the rock they pass through, creating a pot of soft mud. The mud in this pot at Solfatara is 140°F (60°C). Some mud pots are much hotter, while others are cool enough for people to relax and bathe in.

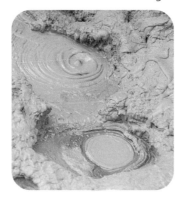 

Crust of tiny sulfur crystals from fumarole in Java, Indonesia

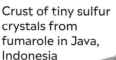

Roman baths

The ancient Romans built huge public baths with hot running water. Baths fed by natural hot springs became medical centers where sick people came to bathe in the mineral-rich water.

Smelly gas

Sulfur crystals can often be seen around fumarole vents. Close to the vent, hot, smelly invisible gases fume. Like steam from a tea kettle, they show up only when the water vapor begins to condense (turn into water) a few centimeters away.

Sleeping beauties

Volcanoes sometimes sleep (lie dormant) for years, or even centuries, between eruptions. In this dormant period, volcanic gases may seep gently from the magma beneath the volcano. As these gases rise through the rocks of the volcano mountain, they react chemically with minerals already in the rocks to create new minerals. These are often brightly colored with large crystals. At Earth's surface, the gases fume gently off into the atmosphere.

Crater lake
Craters often fill with rainwater. This crater lake, on the Shirane volcano in Japan, is very acidic due to gas seeping up from the magma chamber. In an eruption, the acidic water mixed with hot rock and debris could cause a deadly mud flow (pp.56–57).

BIRTH OF A CALDERA

During a large ashy eruption, the empty magma chamber may not be able to support the volcano's slopes. These collapse inward, leaving a huge dip called a caldera.

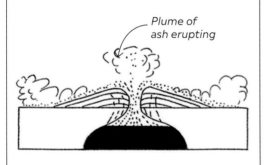

Plume of ash erupting

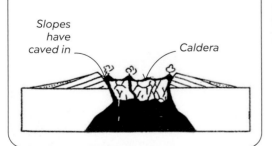

Slopes have caved in

Caldera

Santorini
This Greek island is the rim of a caldera formed by a huge volcanic eruption c. 1620 BCE. The massive explosion may have led to the collapse of the Minoan civilization on the neighboring island of Crete.

Precious stones

Chemicals in the hot volcanic fluids cool slowly inside gas bubbles or in other cavities in the volcanic rock. This process often produces large crystals that can be cut and polished into gemstones. Hard stones, like diamonds, are the most prized because they last forever.

Brightly colored rocks seen by Lord Hamilton at Solfatara (pp.36–37) and illustrated by Pietro Fabris

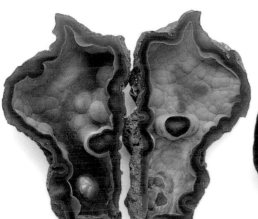

Agate-lined geode (cavity) from Brazil

Agates

These beautiful banded stones form in cavities in cooled or cooling volcanic rocks. Each band is formed at a different time period.

Red Sea gem

Gem-quality olivine is a deep green color. The gem is known as peridot.

Cut peridot

Born in the lava

Zeolite crystals grow in old gas bubbles in lava. They are found in a variety of colors and forms.

Radiating zeolite crystals from the Faëroe Islands

Olivine from St. John's Island in the Red Sea

Uncut diamond in volcanic rock from the mantle, from Kimberley in South Africa

Sleeping volcano

Mount Rainier is one of a chain of volcanoes in the Cascade range in the US. There are no records, but the volcano probably erupted several times in the 1800s. The events can be dated from tree rings, which show stunted growth after an eruption.

Life returns

Volcanic eruptions can have a dramatic effect on the landscape. Volcanic ash is full of nutrients that enrich the soil, but too much can be catastrophic for farmers. Thick, sticky lava covering the land can take months to cool. Decades may pass before plant life returns to the landscape. Only when a rich soil covers the ground is it lush and fertile again. This process may take generations.

Raw lava

Dense, interlocking crystal structure

A few lichens find a home on the lava

Lichen covers the lava, providing a soft surface for other plants

Putting down roots

Ferns, mosses, and lichens are some of the first plants to grow after an eruption. Here, a fern takes root in a ropy pahoehoe lava flow less than a year old on the slopes of Kilauea, Hawaii (pp.18–19).

Gathering moss

The rate at which plants grow back after an eruption depends on the type of erupted material. Plants are slowest in taking root on lava flows; they grow more quickly in ashy, pyroclastic material (p.16). The lava pieces are all from the 1944 aa flow on the west slope of Mount Vesuvius in Italy. Around 47 years later, lichen covers a lot of the flow and moss, grasses, and weedy flowering plants are taking root.

Beginnings of topsoil

Grasses, often the first flowering plants to grow

Rocks and the remains of dead vegetation break down into soil, and grass and moss take root

Lichen cling to exposed parts of rock

Two species of moss grow in thin soil

New cone is still bare ash

Monte Somma, part of caldera (p.38) left by huge, prehistoric eruption

Pine forests cover lower slopes

Mount Vesuvius steaming after mild eruption of 1855

Washed ashore

Seeds blown over or washed up on the beach of Surtsey (left) soon took root in nearby ashfields.

Birth of an island

In November 1963, an undersea eruption off southwest Iceland gave birth to a new island, Surtsey (p.20).

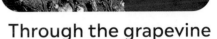

Through the grapevine

The land around Vesuvius has been fertilized by ash from regular eruptions over the last 2,000 years. Grapes grown in the lush soil are used to make wine.

Peacock butterfly lives on nectar of flowering plants

Eventually, the soil is thick enough to support larger plants

Weedy flowering plant

Flower of Lydia

This shrub, a kind of broom, is one of the first plants to grow on the lava from Mount Vesuvius in Italy.

Roman amphorae

The stacks of amphorae for strong wine and olive oil found at Pompeii (pp.26-31) show how fertile the soil was in Roman times.

Lacrima Christi

Mount Vesuvius is shown on the label of this wine grown on the volcano's slopes. Without the nutrients from the volcanic ash, the vines would not grow so thickly and the wine would taste less sweet.

41

Studying volcanoes

Volcanologists—scientists who watch, record, and interpret volcanoes—spend years monitoring volcanoes to try and predict when and how they will next erupt. Most of their work involves analyzing data, but fieldwork on the slopes of active volcanoes is vital. This involves taking lava and gas samples and measuring changes in the shape of landforms and temperature—usually while wearing protective clothing.

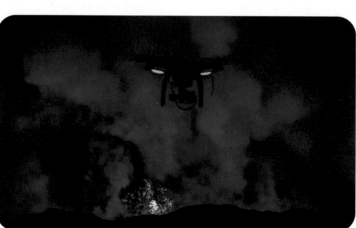

Overhead view

A drone is seen here flying over the 2014 eruption at Bardarbunga, a volcano in Iceland. While drones offer a spectacular view of volcanic eruptions, there have been cases of them melting or crashing when they fly too close.

Spaced-out suit

This protective suit has a metal coating that reflects the heat of the volcano and leaves the person inside cool. Heat-proof boots are worn to walk across the red-hot lava.

Volcano notebook

The volcanologist makes notes and sketches of everything that takes place during an eruption. The significance of some things may only become clear later.

Hot rod

This metal rod is ideal for collecting red-hot lava. The volcanologist dips the end into the lava flow, then twists it around, hooking up a blob of lava.

Hard hat

Thermometer used to check lava temperature can read up to 482°F (250°C)

GPS tracking

GPS data can be used to monitor volcanoes. Several receivers, like the one shown here, are placed around a volcano to form a GPS network. The combined data they record helps scientists track any tiny movements on the volcano's surface due to magma movement underneath.

Too hot to handle

Volcanologists wear asbestos gloves to pick up red-hot lava. Hard hats protect against volcanic bombs (p.18).

Gloves made from the heat-resistant mineral asbestos

Pathfinder

This mining transit is a useful tool for mapping the ground of a volcano. It has a compass and a level (to find verticals and horizontals). Small and light, it can be clipped onto the volcanologist's belt.

Level

Compass

Rotating stage

Folding, portable tripod

Mapping the moving Earth

A precise level is used to detect the small changes in ground level that occur before an eruption.

Other planets

The many space missions over the past few decades have brought back photographs of volcanic activity on other planets. Like Earth, the Moon, Venus, and Mars have surfaces that have been partly shaped by volcanic activity. The volcanoes on the Moon and Mars have been extinct for many millions of years. Scientists suspect that Venus's volcanoes may still be active. But of all the other planets in our solar system, only a few—Io, one of Jupiter's 79 moons, and a few moons of Neptune and Saturn—show active volcanoes.

👁 **EYEWITNESS**

Moon monitoring
Dr. Rosaly Lopes is a planetary scientist who was part of the Galileo Flight Project—a mission to Jupiter. She observed Jupiter's volcanic moon Io from 1996 to 2001 and discovered 71 active volcanoes on it. After working on the Cassini mission to Saturn (2002–2018), Lopes has studied the geology of Titan, Saturn's largest moon.

Volcano on Mars
The extinct volcano Olympus Mons is 373 miles (600 km) across and rises 16 miles (25 km) above the surrounding plain. It is the largest volcano to be found in the universe so far. Huge calderas (p.38) nest inside another at its summit.

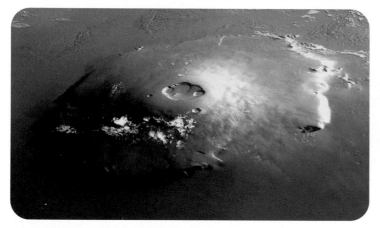

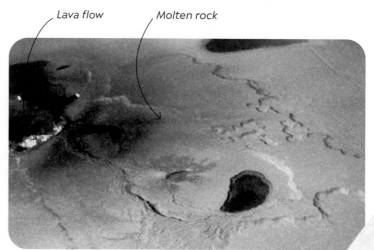

Lava flow   *Molten rock*

Surface of Io
This colored infrared image shows a volcanic region on the surface of Io. The image shows molten rock and a 37-mile- (60-km-) long lava flow, produced by a volcanic eruption.

Beneath the clouds
The spacecraft *Magellan* used imaging radar to penetrate the dense atmosphere of Venus. The images revealed huge volcanoes lurking beneath the clouds. They were named after women, including goddesses from mythology.

Volcano Gula

Volcano Sif

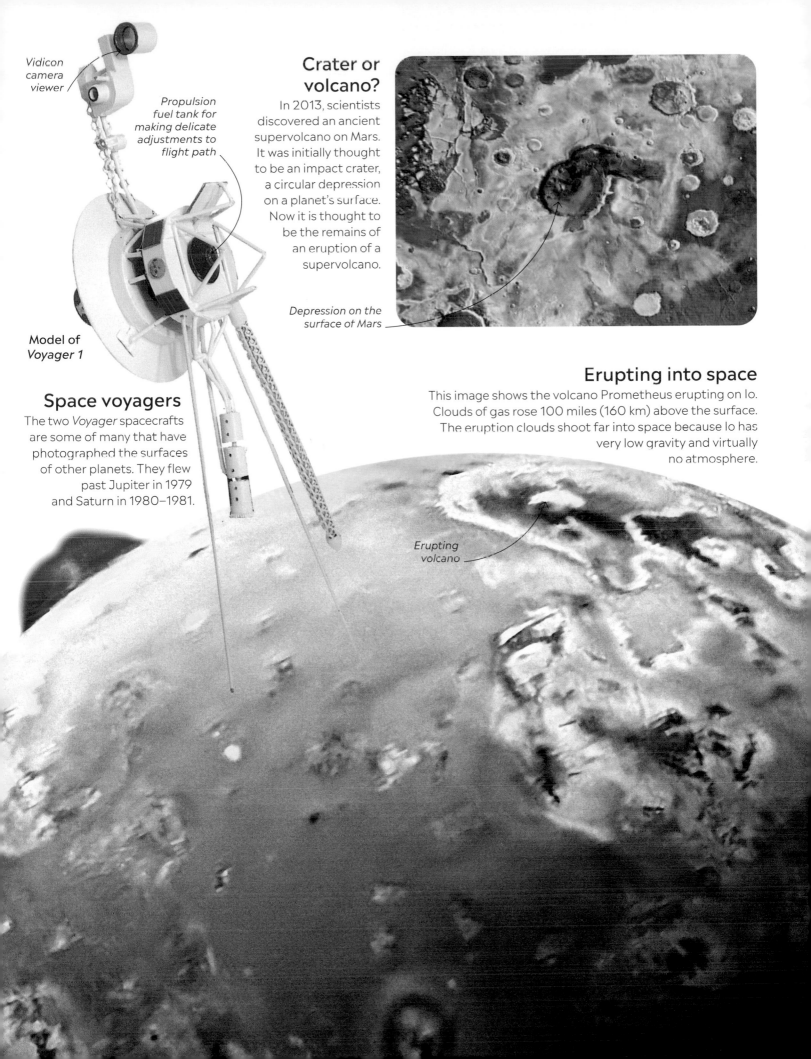

Vidicon camera viewer

Propulsion fuel tank for making delicate adjustments to flight path

Model of *Voyager 1*

Crater or volcano?

In 2013, scientists discovered an ancient supervolcano on Mars. It was initially thought to be an impact crater, a circular depression on a planet's surface. Now it is thought to be the remains of an eruption of a supervolcano.

Depression on the surface of Mars

Space voyagers

The two *Voyager* spacecrafts are some of many that have photographed the surfaces of other planets. They flew past Jupiter in 1979 and Saturn in 1980–1981.

Erupting into space

This image shows the volcano Prometheus erupting on Io. Clouds of gas rose 100 miles (160 km) above the surface. The eruption clouds shoot far into space because Io has very low gravity and virtually no atmosphere.

Erupting volcano

1906 cartoon, captioned "I hope I never have one of those splitting headaches again."

When the earth moves

Being in a large earthquake is a terrifying experience. When the shaking starts, there is no knowing how long it will go on or how severe it will be. The longest tremor ever recorded, the Alaskan earthquake of March 23, 1964, lasted four minutes. But most quakes last less than a minute. In those brief moments, homes, stores, and even entire cities are destroyed. Great cracks may appear in the ground during the quake. Aftershocks, which follow a big tremor, can continue for months.

Disaster movie

This earthquake movie was shown in "Sensurround"—low-frequency sounds meant to simulate earthquake shaking.

Shaken up

The Roman philosopher Seneca wrote about the earthquake that damaged Pompeii in 62 CE. He was particularly interested in the psychological effects of the ground shaking and the natural fear it caused.

Panic sets in

People leave buildings and rush into the streets in panic as an earthquake shakes the city of Valparaiso, Chile, in 1906.

Solid as a rock?

This piece of limestone has a natural polish caused by earthquake stresses and strains. The flat surface was almost melted by the heat generated as the rock broke.

Folded

This book was damaged in an earthquake that devastated Skopje in Yugoslavia in 1963. Skopje sits on the site of the ancient city of Scupi, which was completely flattened by an earthquake in 518 CE.

Shaking, fire, and flood

The 1755 quake destroyed three-quarters of Lisbon's buildings. Huge tsunamis (pp.56–57) destroyed the harbor, and more than 10,000 people were killed.

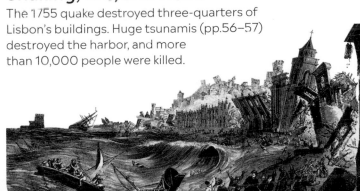

Shaken to the foundations

An earthquake of 6.4 magnitude struck Taiwan in 2018. It caused many residential buildings like this one to partially collapse.

👁 EYEWITNESS

Voltaire (1694–1778)
The 1755 Lisbon earthquake made Europeans wonder about disaster. French philosopher Voltaire reacted deeply to the 1755 Lisbon earthquake, calling it an "appalling spectacle of woe." In his novel *Candide*, he made fun of religious figures who said that God was punishing Lisbon residents for their immoral ways.

Cracking ground

Volcanic tremors are caused by moving magma. Here, rising magma has cracked the ground before an eruption of Piton de la Fournaise volcano, Réunion. Solid rocks can fracture when the earth shakes. This road cracked during an earthquake measuring 6.9 on the Richter scale (pp.48–49).

Fallen building rubble as a result of the earthquake

Intensity and magnitude

How do you measure the size of an earthquake? News reports usually give the quake a magnitude on the Richter scale. The Richter magnitude is useful because it can be worked out from a recording—called a seismogram—of the earthquake waves (pp.52–55). These waves can be recorded from anywhere on the planet.

The intensity of the shaking and how it affects buildings and people cannot be recorded by a machine. It is calculated by inspecting damage and measured on a scale such as the Modified Mercalli Intensity Scale.

Giuseppe Mercalli
(1850–1914)

Intensity

The Italian volcanologist Giuseppe Mercalli created his intensity scale in 1902. He used 12 grades with Roman numerals—12 being a total catastrophe.

I The shaking is not felt by people, but instruments record it.

II People at rest notice the shaking (above), especially if they are on upper floors of buildings. Lightly suspended objects may swing.

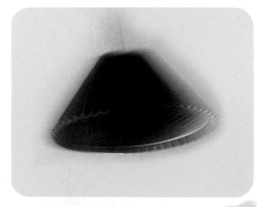

III People indoors feel a vibration like the passing of a light truck. Hanging objects start to swing (above).

IV Vibration like a heavy truck passing. Dishes rattle and standing cars rock.

V Felt outdoors. Dishes and windows break. Small objects, like a glass with liquid, fall.

Magnitude

In the 1930s, Charles Richter wanted to compare the sizes of local earthquakes. First, he calculated the distance between himself and the earthquake. He then used this distance, together with the wiggly tracings of the ground movement (pp.52-55), to come up with the magnitude.

People fleeing from an earthquake in panic

Recording shakes

Richter took the smallest earthquake he could record at the time and called it magnitude zero. The highest Richter magnitudes recorded are about 9.

 EYEWITNESS

The Richter scale

American seismologist Charles Richter (1900–1985) developed the Richter scale that is widely used for measuring earthquake magnitude. He advocated better building codes and earthquake preparedness.

MAPPING QUAKES

This map shows contours for an earthquake that struck Japan on May 22, 1925. Deeper reds indicate strongest intensities.

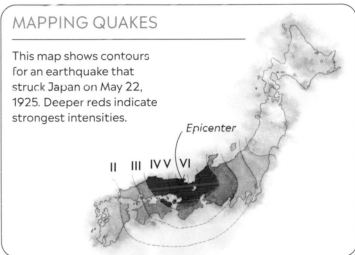

Epicenter

II III IV V VI

VI Felt by all. Many are frightened and rush outdoors. People walk unsteadily; heavy furniture moves (above).

VII Moderate damage in well-built buildings. Severe damage in poorly designed buildings.

VIII Partial collapse of badly designed buildings. Falling chimneys, steeples. Cracks in wet ground. Heavy furniture topples over.

IX Extensive damage in most building types. Frame buildings, if not bolted down, shift off their foundations (above).

X Masonry and frame buildings destroyed (above). Some well-built wooden buildings destroyed. Large landslides. Water thrown out of rivers.

Shock waves

Earthquake waves travel fast—about 15,500 mph (25,000 kph) in rock. In the seconds after the rock fracture that causes the earthquake, shock waves travel out in all directions. Usually, they are most devastating near the epicenter—the place on Earth's surface nearest to where the rocks have fractured. But sometimes the waves are slowed down by soft sands and muds. This can cause severe shaking even far from the epicenter.

Seismogram

This is a recording of a 5.1 magnitude quake. The primary (P) waves arrive first, followed by slower secondary (S) waves. The time lag between the P and S waves—17 seconds—is used to calculate the distance from the epicenter.

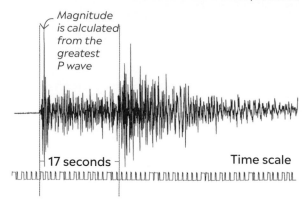

Magnitude is calculated from the greatest P wave

17 seconds

Time scale

First P wave   First S wave

EPICENTER

In 1989, seismologists (people who study earthquakes) in Scotland, Africa, and India calculated how far away a quake had struck and drew a circle across the globe based on their results. The circles met in the Caspian Sea, the epicenter of the quake.

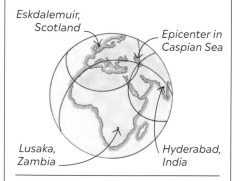

Eskdalemuir, Scotland

Epicenter in Caspian Sea

Lusaka, Zambia

Hyderabad, India

DEEP FOCUS

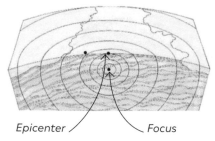

Epicenter   *Focus*

An earthquake's focus—the area where the rocks have fractured—is usually many miles inside Earth.

Living through an earthquake

This model shows the waves from a large earthquake. The fast P waves (yellow) are about to strike the area on the far left. S waves (blue) follow, causing considerable damage. The slowest, surface waves (red), arrive seconds later, causing the total collapse of buildings already weakened by the S waves.

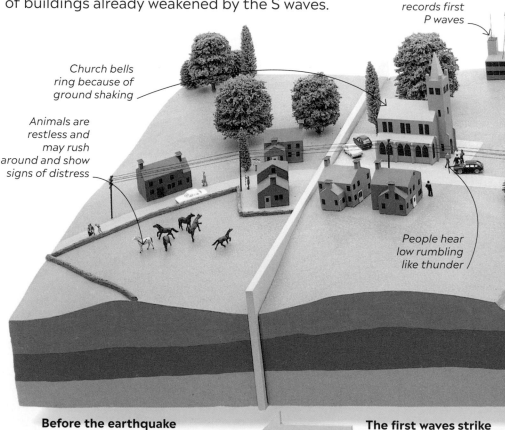

Seismic station records first P waves

Church bells ring because of ground shaking

Animals are restless and may rush around and show signs of distress

People hear low rumbling like thunder

Before the earthquake
Animals often sense something is wrong in the minutes before an earthquake strikes.

P waves

The first waves strike
The first P waves may be so small, they are heard but not felt.

Devastated in a minute

In 1843, the town of Pointe-à-Pitre on the island of Guadeloupe was hit by an earthquake of magnitude 8. The shaking lasted for about a minute—long enough to reduce most of the buildings to ruins. A fire that followed destroyed what was left of the town.

Houses destroyed in the earthquake

High-rise building in Turkey damaged by a 7.0 magnitude earthquake in 2020

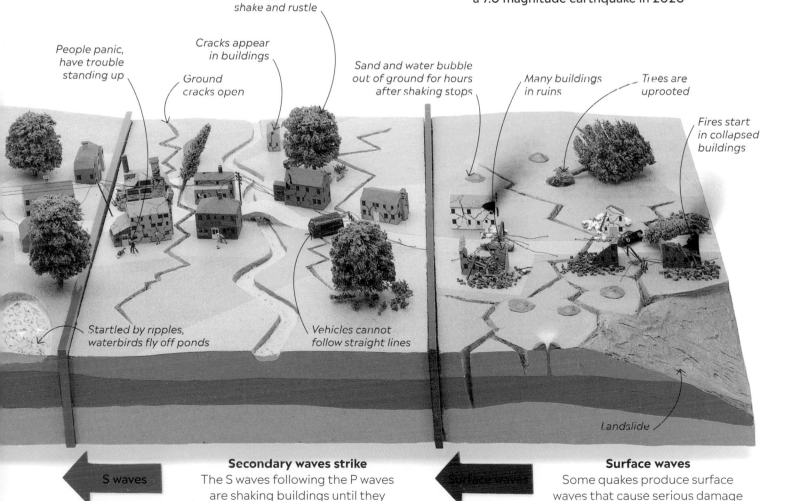

Trees and bushes shake and rustle

Cracks appear in buildings

People panic, have trouble standing up

Ground cracks open

Sand and water bubble out of ground for hours after shaking stops

Many buildings in ruins

Trees are uprooted

Fires start in collapsed buildings

Startled by ripples, waterbirds fly off ponds

Vehicles cannot follow straight lines

Landslide

S waves

Secondary waves strike
The S waves following the P waves are shaking buildings until they crack or collapse.

Surface waves

Surface waves
Some quakes produce surface waves that cause serious damage far from the epicenter.

Measuring earthquakes

The first instrument for recording earthquakes was built by the Chinese scientist Zhang Heng in the 2nd century CE. The device, known as a seismoscope, could record earthquakes too slight to be noticed otherwise. In 1856, a more sophisticated device was invented by the Italian Luigi Palmieri. His seismograph was designed to measure the overall size of the earthquake shaking (pp.48–49).

Early seismologist

The Chinese were keeping lists of earthquakes as early as 780 BCE. But it was not until 132 CE that the Chinese astronomer Zhang Heng (78–139) invented the first seismoscope. The bronze device measured about 6.6 ft (2 m) across.

Suspension mechanism pulls on dragon's mouth

Pendulum

Inner workings of Zhang Heng's seismoscope

Seismoscope

During a tremor, the vessel moves more than the heavy pendulum hanging inside. This triggers one or more of the dragons to open their jaws and release a bronze ball into the mouths of the toads below.

Ball held in dragon's mouth

The toad that is farthest from the epicenter catches the falling ball. This indicates which direction the quake came from.

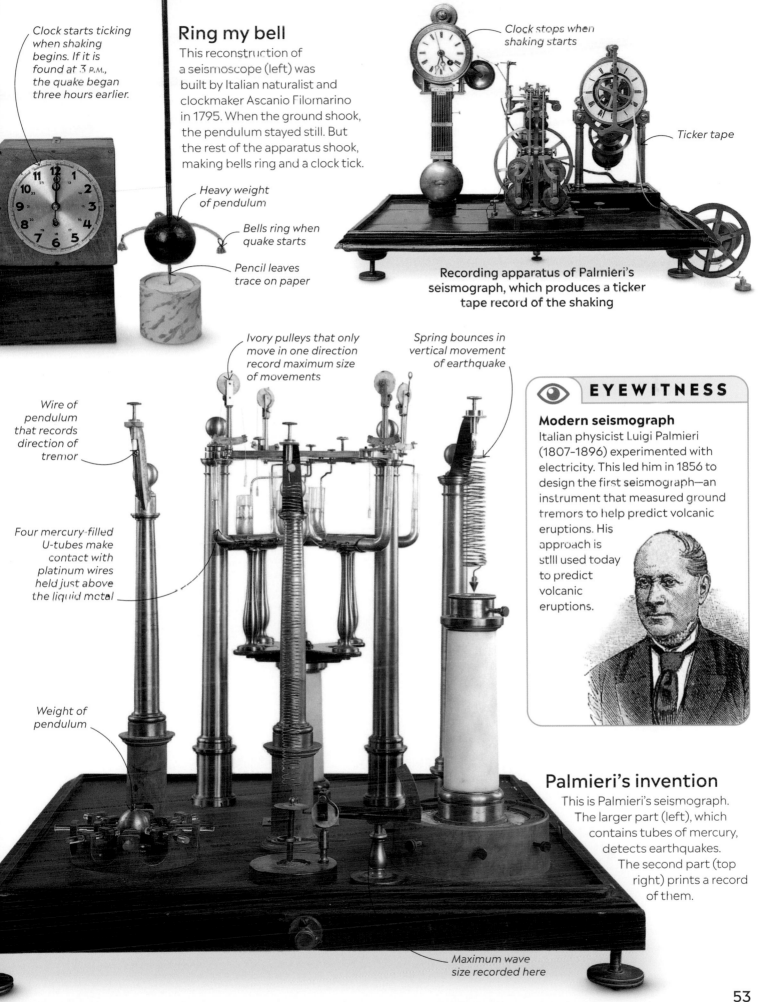

Clock starts ticking when shaking begins. If it is found at 3 P.M., the quake began three hours earlier.

Ring my bell

This reconstruction of a seismoscope (left) was built by Italian naturalist and clockmaker Ascanio Filomarino in 1795. When the ground shook, the pendulum stayed still. But the rest of the apparatus shook, making bells ring and a clock tick.

Heavy weight of pendulum

Bells ring when quake starts

Pencil leaves trace on paper

Clock stops when shaking starts

Ticker tape

Recording apparatus of Palmieri's seismograph, which produces a ticker tape record of the shaking

Ivory pulleys that only move in one direction record maximum size of movements

Spring bounces in vertical movement of earthquake

Wire of pendulum that records direction of tremor

Four mercury-filled U-tubes make contact with platinum wires held just above the liquid metal

Weight of pendulum

Palmieri's invention

This is Palmieri's seismograph. The larger part (left), which contains tubes of mercury, detects earthquakes. The second part (top right) prints a record of them.

Maximum wave size recorded here

Seismometers

Seismometers capture earthquake movement. They work on the principle that an earthquake shakes a heavy pendulum less than the surrounding ground.

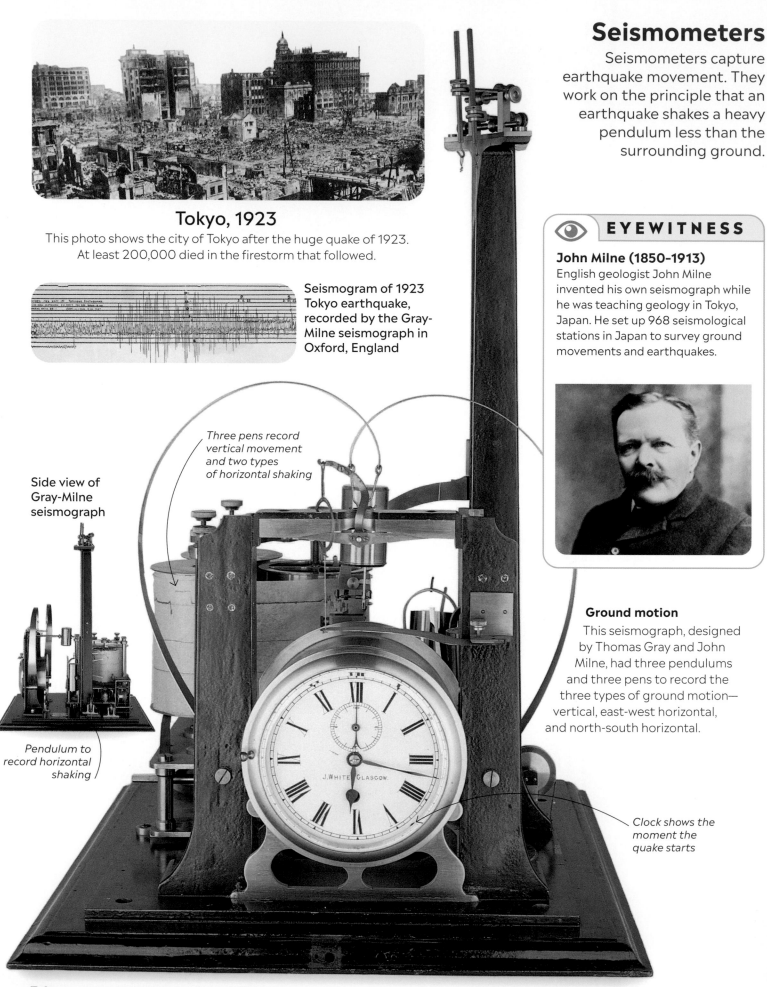

Tokyo, 1923

This photo shows the city of Tokyo after the huge quake of 1923. At least 200,000 died in the firestorm that followed.

Seismogram of 1923 Tokyo earthquake, recorded by the Gray-Milne seismograph in Oxford, England

Three pens record vertical movement and two types of horizontal shaking

Side view of Gray-Milne seismograph

Pendulum to record horizontal shaking

Ground motion

This seismograph, designed by Thomas Gray and John Milne, had three pendulums and three pens to record the three types of ground motion—vertical, east-west horizontal, and north-south horizontal.

J.WHITE GLASGOW.

Clock shows the moment the quake starts

A modern observatory

At the Sinabung Volcano Observatory in Indonesia, a seismometer measures the ground movement and volcanic activity. Modern seismographs record information digitally, which allows for much better analysis.

Portable

Networks of portable seismometers are used to monitor the aftershocks of big quakes and ground tremors during volcanic eruptions.

Moonquakes

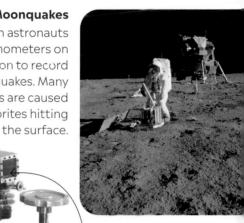

American astronauts left seismometers on the Moon to record moonquakes. Many moonquakes are caused by meteorites hitting the surface.

Case hides suspended pendulum

Paper drum winds very slowly between earthquakes. When shaking starts, gears change and the drum starts feeding the paper through much faster

Handle for winding up weight that turns drum

Suspended weight drives paper drum (mechanical clocks driven in same way)

Damping system, which makes sure that each shock wave is only recorded once

Smoked paper seismogram

Arm from which pendulums are suspended

Heavy duty

This is a restored version of the seismograph invented in 1908 by German scientist Emil Wiechert (1861–1928). Its 440 lb (200 kg) mass measures the two horizontal movements of ground shaking. It worked with a smaller instrument that measured vertical motion.

Smoking up

Early seismographs, many still in use, scratch their traces on smoked paper. This avoids the problem of ink running out—a disaster during tremors.

Mud, fire, and floods

The events that follow an earthquake or volcanic eruption can be even more dangerous than the disaster itself. Heavy rain mixed with volcanic ash can create devastating mud flows. In mountains, both quakes and eruptions may trigger landslides and avalanches. By or beneath the sea, they can both cause giant water waves known as tsunamis.

Overview of Armero mud flow, 1985

Buried in mud

In 1985, the Ruiz volcano in Colombia, South America, spewed clouds of ash and pumice onto snow and ice at the mountain's summit. The melted snow and ash formed a heavy mud flow that traveled at speeds of up to 22 mph (35 kph). In the city of Armero, 37 miles (60 km) away, some 22,000 people were buried alive by the waves of mud, rock, and debris that set around them like wet concrete.

Truck trapped in mud, Armero

Pozzuoli

The town of Pozzuoli near Naples, Italy, has been shaken by many small earthquakes. Part of the town was abandoned after shaking damage in 1983. The town has risen several yards since then, so the harbor had to be rebuilt lower down.

Old mooring post

New dock level

Dwarfing Fuji

Tsunamis are caused by both volcanic eruptions and earthquakes. The volcano Fujiyama in Japan is shown in this picture of a tsunami by Katsushika Hokusai (1760–1849).

Tsunami

In 2011, an earthquake with 9.0 magnitude hit Oshika Peninsula in Japan, causing a tsunami. More than 18,000 people were killed. The tsunami also caused a system failure in the nuclear power plant Fukushima Daiichi. As a result, tons of radioactive water leaked into the Pacific Ocean.

Avalanche

In 2015, an earthquake of magnitude 7.8 hit Nepal. This triggered a massive avalanche on Mount Everest. At least 20 people were killed, making it the deadliest disaster on the mountain. Many others were trapped and injured.

Snow hurtling toward the Everest Base Camp

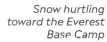

Fire in the ruins

In 2011, a petrochemical plant in Ichihara, Japan, caught fire after a devastating 9.0 magnitude earthquake. The fires that follow quakes or eruptions can destroy cities. If gas mains are broken or inflammable liquids spilled, the lightest spark causes fire. Shaking often damages underground water supply pipes, making a blaze harder to fight.

State of
emergency

The chaos that follows a big earthquake or volcanic eruption makes rescue difficult and dangerous. Half-collapsed buildings may topple further at any moment. Hazardous substances could suddenly catch fire or explode. In ash-flow or mud-flow eruptions, no one knows when to expect another surge. Damage to electricity, gas, and water supplies and disruption to communication links make rescue operations even harder to mount.

Perilous rescue

A survivor is lifted by helicopter in Armero, Colombia, in 1985 (p.56).

Finding live bodies

A thermal imaging camera is used to locate people trapped after an earthquake. Survivors are often buried, wounded or unconscious, in the rubble of their collapsed homes. The camera uses infrared radiation to detect the heat of a living person.

Rescue worker checks disaster site with thermal camera

Thermal imaging camera

THERMAL CAMERA

R
+   B   G   −
P   SET

Muddy escape

A survivor is rescued from the boiling mud flows that engulfed Armero in 1985. Many survivors had to be treated for burns.

Helping out

The London Fire and Civil Defence Authority sends trained teams to disaster zones like northwest Iran after the massive quake of June 1990.

Trapped person detector

This device was used to find people trapped in wreckage after the Armenian earthquake of 1988. The device works by detecting vibrations.

Haiti earthquake

Hundreds of thousands of people were killed in Haiti in January 2010, when a magnitude 7 earthquake hit the country. Many important buildings, such as the Presidential Palace and the National Assembly Building, were badly damaged.

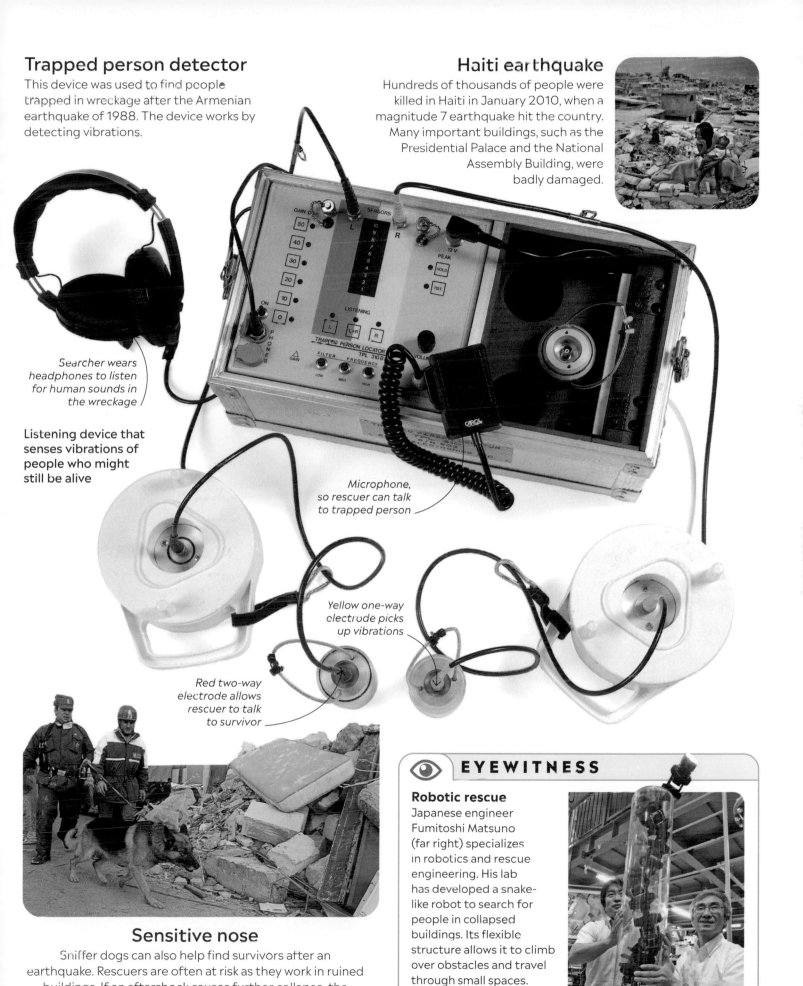

Searcher wears headphones to listen for human sounds in the wreckage

Listening device that senses vibrations of people who might still be alive

Microphone, so rescuer can talk to trapped person

Yellow one-way electrode picks up vibrations

Red two-way electrode allows rescuer to talk to survivor

Sensitive nose

Sniffer dogs can also help find survivors after an earthquake. Rescuers are often at risk as they work in ruined buildings. If an aftershock causes further collapse, the rescuers may have to be rescued, too.

EYEWITNESS

Robotic rescue

Japanese engineer Fumitoshi Matsuno (far right) specializes in robotics and rescue engineering. His lab has developed a snake-like robot to search for people in collapsed buildings. Its flexible structure allows it to climb over obstacles and travel through small spaces.

One step ahead

Italian magazines produced for the 1990s, the International Decade for Natural Disaster Reduction

As the planet's population increases, more people are living in danger zones, along faults or close to active volcanoes. We cannot hope to stop disasters entirely, but we can reduce their number and scale. Learning to live in disaster zones means monitoring volcanoes and fault lines and building cities that can withstand earthquakes. It also means educating people to know what to do in an emergency.

In the shadow of Vesuvius

Two thousand years after the volcano's greatest eruption (pp.30–31), modern Herculaneum (above) is a thriving town.

👁 EYEWITNESS

Resisting quakes
American architect Frank Lloyd Wright (1857–1959) was a pioneer in the design of earthquake-resistant buildings. His Imperial Hotel in Tokyo survived the 1923 quake almost unscathed.

Standing strong

Many modern buildings in earthquake-prone cities are designed to withstand shaking. Taipei 101 in Taiwan contains a giant steel ball at the top that acts like a pendulum to counterbalance earthquakes. Concrete-filled columns inside the tower also make it sturdy enough to withstand strong earthquakes.

Shake 'til they drop

Built in 1923, this Japanese shaking table was used to test models of buildings to see how they stood up to severe shaking.

Falling masonry

In this earthquake drill, rescue workers are treating actors "hit" by falling masonry. Designing buildings without heavy stone ornaments or chimneys might help reduce the numbers of casualties like these.

Most measured place

The town of Parkfield in central California lies above the San Andreas fault system. Seismologists (pp.48-49) have long predicted a major quake here. A laser measuring system is being used to detect movements along the fault. It can detect ground movement of less than a millimeter over a distance of 3.7 miles (6 km).

Earthquake drill

In Japan and the Philippines, earthquake drills are part of everyday life. Children learn to keep a flashlight and shoes by their beds so they can get to safety at night. The safest place indoors is under a piece of furniture like a table, or beneath a door frame.

Learning from the past

Earthquakes of the same size tend to happen in the same place at regular intervals. Studying large quakes—in this case, one that rocked Italy in 2009—may help scientists predict the next big tremor.

Measuring creep

A technician for the US Geological Survey has been measuring creep— slow movement along the fault.

Anger of the gods

As long as people have lived on Earth, they have been curious about natural events like volcanic eruptions and earthquakes. Myths and legends are a way of recording or explaining these strange happenings. For centuries, many societies have explained natural events as the workings of a god or gods. It was thought that angry gods would punish people with a fiery eruption or the horrible shaking of an earthquake. Some societies still believe that certain gods live on the eerie summits of volcanoes, which are often shrouded in fire and cloud.

Popocatépetl

This Aztec illustration shows Popocatépetl in Mexico. When the volcano erupted violently in the 1520s, the Aztecs believed it was because the gods were angry with the Spanish conquerors who had looted their temples.

Flames and volcanic plumes rising into the air

Christians in Naples, Italy, try to stop the 1906 eruption of Mount Vesuvius (p.31) with crosses and prayers

Poseidon's trident

Shaking the seafloor

When the Greek sea god Poseidon was angry, he banged the seafloor with his trident (spear). The ancient Greeks believed that this led to earthquakes and tsunamis (pp.56–57).

In the **Greek epic *Odyssey*,** **Poseidon stirred up storms and strong waves at sea.**

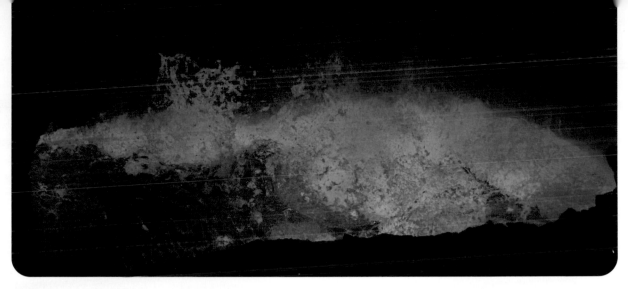

Human sacrifice

Centuries ago in Nicaragua, people used to throw young women into the lava lake at Masaya to stop the volcano from erupting.

Responsible frog

Many cultures believed that the ground they stood on was held up by some huge creature. The Mongolians believed this was a gigantic frog. Each time the animal stumbled under his great burden, the ground shook with an earthquake.

When the gods are away ...

A Japanese myth says earthquakes were caused by a giant catfish. Normally, the fish was pinned down by a large rock. But when the gods were away, the creature could escape. This print shows the gods flying back after a big quake, carrying a rock.

Master of fire

The ancient Greeks believed the god Hephaistos had his fiery workshops under volcanoes. Another god, Prometheus, stole some of the fire from the volcanoes and gave it to humans.

Bronze figure of Hephaistos, 1st or 2nd century BCE

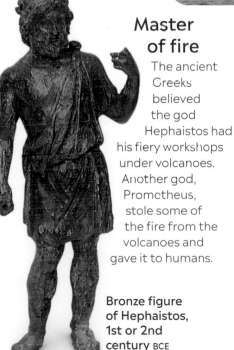

Home of the gods

Mount Fuji in Japan is thought to be the home of the god Kunitokotache. The sacred spirit of the mountain, Fujiyama, is said to protect the Japanese people.

Sodom and Gomorrah

According to the Bible, God destroyed these cities with flood and fire because the inhabitants were evil.

One-eyed giant

From above, the craters on Mount Vesuvius look like giant eyes. They may have inspired the Greek myth of the Cyclops, a tribe of one-eyed giants who helped the fire god Hephaistos (left).

Did you **know?**

AMAZING FACTS

Much of New Zealand's North Island, and all island life, were devastated by the eruption of the Lake Taupo caldera in 180 CE. Luckily, the first human inhabitants did not occupy the island until 1000 CE.

Around 200 black bears were killed in the eruption of Mount St. Helens.

Figures from Mount St. Helens estimate that 11,000 hares; 6,000 deer; 5,200 elk; 1,400 coyotes; 300 bobcats; and 15 mountain lions were killed by the blast.

Pyroclastic flows can travel at up to 311 mph (500 kph) and reach temperatures of 1,472°F (800°C), burning everything in their path.

Where cracks form in the ocean floor, the water heated by magma can reach temperatures of 1,224°F (662°C).

One of Iceland's greatest attractions used to be the Great Geyser, near Reykjavik, which had a jet 197–262 ft (60–80 m) high. The geyser stopped spouting in 1916.

When Krakatoa in Indonesia erupted in 1883, the noise was so loud, it burst the eardrums of sailors over 25 miles (40 km) away. Around 36,000 people died, most killed by tsunamis—some 100 ft (30 m) tall—that devastated Java and Sumatra. Villages, ships, and boats were swept inland.

Fires are a major problem after an earthquake. Fractured gas pipes mean fires spread rapidly and burst water mains dry up the hoses. This, together with streets blocked with debris, make the firefighters' work near impossible.

The greatest volcanic eruption in modern times was Tambora, Indonesia, in 1815.

A steamer swept inland at Krakatoa

It produced 19.2 miles^3 (80 km^3) of volcanic ash, compared to 0.24 miles^3 (1 km^3) measured at Mount St. Helens. In the past 10,000 years, only four eruptions have been as violent as Tambora.

A tsunami can travel at speeds of up to 500 mph (805 kph).

Animals often act strangely before an earthquake. In 1975, in China, scientists correctly predicted an earthquake when they noticed snakes waking up from hibernation and rats swarming.

Burning clouds from Pinatubo, Philippines, 1991

Pyroclastic flows traveling at over 40 mph (70 kph) were recorded

QUESTIONS AND ANSWERS

When is a volcano said to be extinct rather than dormant?

A volcano is classified as active if it has erupted within the last few hundred years. It is dormant if it has not erupted in the last few hundred years but has erupted during the last several thousand years. If a volcano has not erupted during the last several thousand years, it is said to be extinct.

Have people ever tried to stop an advancing lava flow?

When the volcano on the Icelandic island of Heimaey erupted in 1973, the residents tried to save the harbor on which the island depended from the lava. They did not stop it, but by spraying 6.6 million tons (6 million tonnes) of seawater at the lava, they slowed it down and slightly altered its course. The lava flow stopped just 450 ft (137 m) from the harbor.

What should you do if there is an earthquake?

Shelter in a doorway or under a strong table and protect your head with your arms.

Earthquake drill at a school in the US

When the tremors stop, leave the building and shelter away from walls, which may collapse.

How many active volcanoes are there in the world?

There are more than 1,500 active volcanoes that rise above sea level. On average, around 20–30 are actually erupting each month. Some of these are volcanoes that erupt continually, like Mauna Loa and Kilauea.

Could lava just come out of a crack in the earth?

Yes. In 1943, in Paricutin in Mexico, a farmer found lava pouring from a crack in his field. Within a day, there was a cone 33 ft (10 m) high. After a year of eruptions, the lava was 1,476 ft (450 m) tall and had engulfed the nearby town.

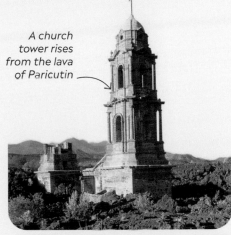
A church tower rises from the lava of Paricutin

Paricutin, Mexico, buried by lava

Mauna Loa, Hawaii

RECORD BREAKERS

- **Biggest volcano**
  Mauna Kea in Hawaii is a massive volcano, 4,446 ft (1,355 m) taller than Mount Everest, but much of it is under the sea.

- **Biggest earthquake**
  In 1960, an earthquake of 9.5 on the Richter scale was recorded in Chile. It caused tsunamis that reached Japan.

- **Highest earthquake death toll**
  In 1556, an earthquake of 8.3 magnitude killed 800,000 people in Shansi, China.

- **Highest tsunami wave**
  The highest tsunami wave following an earthquake was the Indian Ocean tsunami in 2004. The huge waves reached a height of 100 ft (30 m).

- **Largest fault slip**
  The largest ever fault slip was the main cause behind the 2011 tsunami in Japan. The fault in the floor of the North Pacific Ocean slipped by 164 ft (50 m).

Timeline

The timeline below includes just some of the major volcanic eruptions and earthquakes of the past 4,000 years. We have most information about events in living memory or from records in recent history, but volcanologists can look much further back in time by studying the features of Earth's surface.

Gas, dust, and rock explode from Mount St. Helens, 1980

c. 1620 BCE Santorini, Greece
Violent eruptions buried the island of Santorini under 98 ft (30 m) of pumice.

79 CE Vesuvius, Italy
A burning cloud of volcanic ash engulfed the Roman towns of Pompeii and Herculaneum, killing thousands.

Craters mark Skaftar fissure today

1755 Lisbon, Portugal
An earthquake measuring 8.5 on the Richter scale reduced the city to rubble.

1783 Skaftar fires, Iceland
A fissure (crack) 16 miles (27 km) long spewed out poisonous gases and lava.

1815 Tambora, Indonesia
The biggest eruption ever recorded. Around 90,000 people were killed. Volcanic dust reduced levels of sunlight around the world.

1883 Krakatoa, Indonesia
The force of the eruption left a crater 951 ft (290 m) deep in the ocean floor.

1902 Mount Pelée, Martinique
All but two of the entire population of St. Pierre were wiped out by the burning cloud of gas and dust. Around 30,000 people died.

1906 San Francisco, California
Two huge tremors hit the city, setting off fires that burned for many days.

1920 Xining, China
The entire province of Gansu was devastated by the earthquake,

A watch stopped by the eruption of Mount Pelée, 1902

which killed more than 180,000 people.

1923 Tokyo, Japan
An earthquake of 8.3 on the Richter scale flattened 600,000 homes and knocked over stoves, which started a terrible firestorm.

1943 Paricutin, Mexico
Lava flowed from a crack that appeared in a farmer's field. By 1952, the lava cone stood 1,732 ft (528 m) tall.

The ruins of San Francisco, 1906

1963 Surtsey, Iceland
Undersea volcanic explosions created a new island off the southwest coast of Iceland.

1973 Heimaey, Iceland
Eldfell volcano erupted after 5,000 years of dormancy. Molten lava engulfed one-third of the town of Vestmannaeyjar on the Icelandic island of Heimaey.

1976 Tangshan, China
The most disastrous earthquake in modern times. A tremor of 8.3 magnitude killed over 240,000 people.

Cinders engulf Vestmannaeyjar, Iceland

1980 Mount St. Helens, Washington
The eruption of Mount St. Helens devastated vast areas around the volcano.

1985 Mexico City, Mexico
Powerful tremors, measuring 8.1 on the Richter scale, shook Mexico City for three minutes. One million people were left homeless.

1985 Nevado del Ruiz, Colombia
The eruption of the Ruiz volcano caused a massive mudflow that engulfed the town of Armero 37 miles (60 km) away.

1991 Kilauea, Hawaii
Kilauea volcano suddenly produced large quantities of lava that buried 8 miles (13 km) of road and 181 homes.

1991 Pinatubo, Philippines
This was the most violent volcanic eruption of the 20th century. Around 42,000 homes were destroyed, leaving around 200,000 homeless.

1994 Los Angeles, California
The earthquake destroyed nine highways and 11,000 buildings in 30 seconds.

1995 Kobe, Japan
The most powerful earthquake to hit a modern city, measuring 7.2 on the Richter scale.

1998 New Guinea
A violent offshore earthquake caused a 33 ft (10 m) high tsunami, which swept 1.2 miles (2 km) inland. Around 4,500 people died.

2002 Democratic Republic of Congo
About half a million people were forced to leave their homes when rivers of lava flowed from Mount Nyiragongo. The lava destroyed two-fifths of the town of Goma.

2004 Sumatra-Andaman, Indian Ocean
An undersea earthquake triggered a series of tsunamis, killing around 187,000 people.

2005 Pakistan
Also known as the Kashmir earthquake, this violent quake, measuring 7.6 on the Richter scale, killed around 73,000 people and left 33 million homeless.

The destruction of the expressway, Kobe, Japan, 1995

2010 Haiti
A devastating 7.0 magnitude earthquake struck Haiti in January 2010. More than 220,000 people were estimated to have been killed.

2010 Iceland
In March 2010, Eyjafjallajökull volcano in Iceland erupted and disrupted air traffic across Europe for several weeks. An estimated 10 million passengers were affected worldwide.

2011 Japan
A 9.0 magnitude earthquake and tsunami struck Japan in March 2011. About 20,000 people lost their lives.

2015 Nepal
In April 2015, Nepal was struck by a 7.8 magnitude earthquake that killed nearly 9,000 people and made more than 3 million people homeless.

2018 Sulawesi
A 7.5 magnitude earthquake in Sulawesi, Indonesia, triggered a 16–20 ft (5–6 m) high tsunami. Nearly 4,500 people were killed; about 4,500 were injured; and 210,000 were displaced.

Palu, Sulawesi, destroyed after an earthquake and tsunami in 2018

Find out more

Volcanoes are unpredictable and can be extremely dangerous. However, there are volcanic parks all over the world where you can see volcanic features safely. There are also websites where you can find news of the latest eruptions and even watch volcanic activity live.

Yellowstone Park, Wyoming

These tourists are walking through the Norris geyser basin in Yellowstone National Park, Wyoming. Yellowstone lies on a volcanic hot spot and contains volcanic features such as geysers and fumaroles.

The story of an eruption

The remains of the cities of Pompeii and Herculaneum in Italy (pp.26-32) give visitors an insight into both volcanoes and life in Roman times. Both cities were destroyed when Vesuvius erupted in 79 CE, but the volcano is still active—it last erupted in 1944. Visitors can climb up and look into the crater of the volcano.

Bodies of ancient Romans suffocated by the poisonous gases were preserved in the volcanic ash

The ruins of Pompeii lying in the shadow of Vesuvius

PLACES TO VISIT

NATURAL HISTORY MUSEUM, LONDON
• The Earth galleries have displays on volcanoes and earthquakes.

ETNA, VESUVIUS, AND STROMBOLI, ITALY
• These volcanoes can all be climbed with guides, weather and conditions permitting.

THE CANARY ISLANDS
• You can visit the volcano on La Palma and the volcanic landscape of Lanzerote.

ICELAND
• Iceland has over 20 volcanoes but is most famous for its geysers and hot springs.

Runny pahoehoe lava flowing over a cliff made up of layers of lava

Lava flow from Kilauea volcano in Hawaii

Visiting volcanoes

There are national parks worldwide where visitors can see signs of volcanic activity, past and present. In Hawaii, visitors can drive to the rim of the active volcano Kilauea, walk through a lava tube, and see an eruption from a safe distance.

Watching the earth

In the box below, you will find the addresses of some websites with general background information on volcanology and links to lots of specific volcanoes. The Smithsonian Institution produces an online weekly report on volcanic activity worldwide.

Living with a volcano
These children are learning about Sakurajima volcano in Japan. It is one of the most active volcanoes in the world, erupting nearly constantly. Sakurajima is monitored by a volcano observatory, which collects data that helps predict volcanic activity.

Watching from space
This picture, taken by a Space Shuttle, shows thick clouds of ash and dust from the eruption of Kliuchevskoi volcano in Russia in 1994. Volcanic ash clouds can cause pollution and affect climate. They are watched and measured by satellites.

USEFUL WEBSITES

- A general introduction to volcanoes:
  https://volcano.oregonstate.edu/
- Smithsonian Institution report on volcanic activity:
  www.volcano.si.edu
- Collection of articles on earthquakes:
  https://www.usgs.gov/natural-hazards/earthquake-hazards/education
- On how to build a volcano model:
  sciencebob.com/the-erupting-volcano/

Dangerous work
This volcanologist is checking gas samples inside the crater of Mount Erebus, Antarctica. It is dangerous work, and several volcanologists have been killed by unexpected eruptions. There are lots of sites on the Internet where you can learn more about a volcanologist's work and find out how to become one.

Glossary

AA Hawaiian word to describe thick lava that forms angular lumps when cool.

AFTERSHOCKS Smaller earth tremors that happen after an earthquake. These may occur weeks after the main tremor.

ASH AND DUST The smallest fragments of lava formed when a volcano explodes. Small pieces are called ash, and the powder-fine particles are known as dust.

BASALT Dark, fine-grained volcanic rock, formed by runny lavas. Basalt is the most common volcanic rock.

BLACK SMOKER A volcanic hot spring on the ocean floor that spits out black water rich in minerals.

BOMBS AND BLOCKS Large pieces of lava thrown out during a volcanic eruption. Bombs are slightly rounded, while blocks are more angular.

CALDERA A giant, bowl-shaped crater at the top of a volcano, formed when the summit collapses into the volcano's magma chamber.

CARBONIZE To turn to carbon. Objects that contain carbon will turn to carbon (or charcoal), rather than burn, when there is not enough oxygen available for them to burn in the usual way.

Carbonized walnuts from Pompeii

The crater of Mount Vesuvius, Italy

A red-hot flow of aa lava, Hawaii

CORE Earth's center, made up of dense metals—in particular, iron. The inner core is solid, while the outer core is liquid metal.

CRATER A hollow dip formed when the cone of a volcano collapses inward.

CRATER LAKE Lake formed when water fills the crater or caldera of a volcano. Also known as lava lake.

DORMANT The term used to describe a volcano that has not been active for more than several hundred years but was active within the last several thousand years.

EPICENTER The point on Earth's surface directly above the focus, or point of origin, of an earthquake.

EXTINCT The term used to describe a volcano that has not been active for more than several thousand years.

FAULT A fracture in rock where blocks of rock slide past each other.

FEEDER PIPE The long tube through which magma passes to reach the surface.

FISSURE A crack in the earth. A fissure eruption is one where runny lava flows from the crack.

A geyser in Iceland

FOCUS The point within Earth's mantle from which an earthquake originates.

FUMAROLE A vent or opening in Earth's surface that releases steam or gas.

GEOLOGY The study of the history and development of Earth's rocks. The people who study geology are geologists.

GEYSER A place where water that has been superheated by hot magma bursts up into the air.

HOT SPOT A place in the middle of a tectonic plate, rather than at the boundary, where columns of magma from the mantle rise up through the crust creating a volcano.

HYDROTHERMAL VENT A place where mineral-rich water heated by hot magma underground erupts onto the surface. Geysers, black smokers, and hot springs are all hydrothermal vents.

IGNEOUS ROCKS Rocks formed as hot magma and lava cool.

INTENSITY The term used to describe the severity of the shaking experienced during an earthquake. It is usually measured using the Modified Mercalli Intensity Scale.

LAPILLI Small fragments of lava, formed as the magma bursts out of a volcano.

LAVA Hot, molten rock that erupts from a volcano.

LAVA TUBE A tunnel of lava created when the surface of a lava flow cools and hardens to form a roof, while hot, molten lava continues to flow inside it.

MAGMA Hot, molten rock from within Earth.

MAGMA CHAMBER Area beneath a volcano where magma builds up before an eruption.

MAGNITUDE The term used to describe the severity or scale of an earthquake. This is measured in several ways, the most common of which is the Richter scale.

MANTLE The layer between Earth's crust and its core. The mantle is 1,800 miles (2,900 km) thick.

MERCALLI SCALE The scale for measuring the intensity of an earthquake by observing its effects.

MID-OCEAN RIDGE A mountain ridge on the ocean floor formed where two tectonic plates meet.

MUDFLOW A fast-moving stream of mud, water, and often volcanic ash and pumice.

P WAVES The fastest and first or "primary" waves of an earthquake.

PAHOEHOE The Hawaiian term for hot, runny lava that flows quickly and, usually, in quite shallow flows.

PILLOW LAVA Rounded lava formations shaped when lava erupts gently underwater.

PLATE TECTONICS The theory that Earth's surface is broken up into large slabs or plates that are moving constantly at the rate of a few centimeters a year. Most volcanoes and earthquakes are found at the boundaries of these plates.

PUMICE Lightweight volcanic rock filled with holes formed by the bubbles of gas in the lava.

PYROCLASTIC FLOW A burning cloud of gas, dust, ash, rocks, and bombs that flows down the mountain after an explosive eruption. If the cloud is made up of more gas than ash, it is known as a pyroclastic surge.

RICHTER SCALE Scale for measuring the total energy released by earthquakes and recorded by seismographs. The scale ranges from 1 to 10, with 10 at the most severe end of the scale.

RING OF FIRE The area encircling the Pacific Ocean where most volcanic and earthquake activity occurs.

S WAVES The slower, "secondary" waves of an earthquake.

SEISMIC WAVES The vibrations, or shock waves, that radiate out from the focus of an earthquake.

SEISMOGRAM The record produced by a seismograph, showing the pattern of shock waves from an earthquake.

Pumice

Aa lava

Pahoehoe lava

Seismogram of the 1923 Tokyo earthquake

SEISMOMETER A machine for detecting earthquake shock waves. The machine that records the data is a seismograph.

SUBDUCTION ZONE The area where two tectonic plates meet and one plate is pushed down into the mantle, partly melting rocks. The resulting magma erupts at the surface through volcanoes.

TSUNAMI Fast-moving waves caused by earthquakes or volcanic eruptions that displace the ocean floor and water.

VENT The opening through which a volcanic eruption occurs.

VOLCANOLOGIST A scientist who studies volcanoes.

Volcanologists collecting gas samples on Colima volcano, in Mexico

Index

Acknowledgments

The publisher would like to thank the following people for their help with making the book:
John Lepine and Jane Insley of the Science Museum, London; Robert Symes, Colin Keates, and Tim Parmenter of the Natural History Museum, London; the staff at the Museo Archeologico di Napoli; Giuseppe Luongo, Luigi Iadicicco, and Vincenzo D' Errico at the Vesuvius Observatory for help in photographing the instruments on pp. 49, 53, and 55; Paul Arthur; Paul Cole; Lina Ferrante at Pompeii; Dott. Angarano at Solfatara; Carlo Illario at Herculaneum; Roger Musson of the British Geological Survey; Joe Cann; Tina Chambers for extra photography; Gin von Noorden and Helena Spiteri for editorial assistance; Hazel Beynon for text editing; Céline Carez for research and development; Wilfred Wood and Earl Neish for design assistance; Neville Graham, Sue Nicholson, and Susan St. Louis for the wallchart; Ashok Kumar and Vijay Kandwal for DTP assistance; Saloni Singh and Priyanka Sharma-Saddi for the jacket; Ann Baggaley for proofreading; and Helen Iddles for the index.

Illustrations: John Woodcock

Maps: Sallie Alane Reason

Models: David Donkin (pp. 8–9, 50–51) and Edward Laurence Associates (pp. 12–13)

The publisher would like to thank the following for their kind permission to reproduce their images:

(Key: a-above; b-below; c-centre; f-far; l-left; r-right; t=top; m=middle)

Alamy Stock Photo: FLHC 30: 7c; Marco Isler / Mauritius images GmbH 16c; Erlend Haarberg / Nature Picture Library 21r; Alex Ramsay 28tc; Architecture2000 35br; David Hayes 40cr; Paul Rushton 41bl; Arctic Images 42cb; EFE News Agency 44cra; Imaginechina Limited 46–47b; World History Archive 49clb; Robert Paul van Beets 49bc; Nabaraj Regmi (49bc/House image); Tommy E Trenchard 49br; US Air Force Photo 57c; P. Tu Sherpa / M. Bogati / ZUMA Press 57br; NESTOR BACHMANN / DPA Picture Alliance Archive 61cl; Science History Images 62br; SOPA Images Limited 67b. **B.F.I.:** 46cl. **Bridgeman Art Library:** 6br & tc. **British Museum:** 27bl. **Herge/Casterman:** 20bl. **Dr Joe Cann, University of Leeds:** 25cla. **Jean-Loup Charmet:** 31tl, 46bl, 50–51b. **Circus World Museum, Baraboo, Wisconsin:** 32cra. **Corbis:** Bettmann 67cl; Danny Lehman 65cr; Vittoriano Rastelli 70tc; Roger Ressmeyer 71br. **Eric Crichton:** 41tr. **Culver Pictures Inc:** 60c. **DK Images:** Satellite Imagemap © 1996–2003 Planetary Visions 9c. **Dreamstime.com:** Designua 11c; Adriano Spano 30tr; Damien Verrier 32b; Neirfy 38br; Tawatchai Wanasri 38t; Aaron Hinckley 39b; Ammentorp 48bl; Gaspert 58bl; Robbin Lee 60–61b; Luciano Mortula 63cr. **Earthquake Research Institute, University of Tokyo:** 63cl. **Edimedia/Russian Museum, Leningrad:** 28cl. **E.T. Archive:** 49tr, 58cr, 62clb. **Getty Images:** Romeo Gacad 17br; Marc Szeglat / Barcroft Media 19b; Ron Bull / Toronto Star 23tc; Dana Stephenson 24cr; Mario Laporta / AFP 27br; Atlantide Phototravel / Corbis 30cla; Mohamad Haghani / Stocktrek Images 34cr; Bentley Archive / Popperfoto 41tl; George Rose 42tr; Yasin Akgul / AFP 51tr; Science & Society Picture Library 54cr; Jacques Langevin / Sygma 56tr; Sankei 57clb; Kyodo News 59br; Chip Somodevilla 59tr; JOEL NITO / AFP 61cra; Marc Szeglat / Barcroft Media 63tr. **Getty Images/iStock:** OlegAlbinsky 27tr; Jpgfactory 49bl;

Bestgreenscreen 58bc. **Mary Evans Picture Library:** 8tc, 16tl, 28cr, 46tl, 64tr, 66br. **Le Figaro Magazine/Philippe Bourseiller:** 19t, 19cl, 19cl, 35tl. **G.S.F.:** 13tl, 15tr; /Frank Fitch: 20t. **John Guest c.NASA:** 44b. **Robert Harding Picture Library:** 12tl, 14tl, 15br, 17tr, 20br, 21br, 43br, Explorer 66bl. **Historical Pictures Service, Inc.:** 10br. **Michael Holford:** 22b. **Illustrated London News:** 60crb. **ImageState:** 68bc. **Katz Pictures:** Alberto Garcia/Saba 64b. **Frank Lane Picture Agency:** 23l, 23cr. **Frank Lane Picture Agency/S.Jonasson:** 41ca, 49cr. **Archive Larousse-Giraudon:** 32cl. **Mansell Collection:** 31tr. **NASA:** 24tl; JPL / Goddard 45tr; Science@NASA 55cra. **Natural History Museum:** 34clb. **National Maritime Museum:** 8tl. **Orion Press:** 6bl. **Oxford Scientific Films/Colin Monteath:** 69br; /NASA: 69cl; /Kim Westerkov: 11bl; 15bl. Planet Earth Pictures/Franz J.Camenzind: 7bl; /James D. Watt: 23lcb; /Robert Hessler: 25cr. **Popperfoto:** 6–7t, 11tr, 54tl. **R.C.S. Rizzoli:** 48lc. **Rex Features:** 67tr. **Gary Rosenquist:** 14cl, 14–15c, 14bl, 15cr. **Scala:** Louvre: 63bl. **Science Photo Library:** Gary Hincks 10cr; Martin Rietze 18cr; NOAA 25tr; Martin Rietze 55tl **Science Photo Library/Earth Satellite Corp.:** 6cl; /Peter Menzel: 7br, 21tl, 65bl; /David Parker: 13tr, 60cb, 61crb, 65tc; /Ray Fairbanks: 18cl; /Matthew Shipp: 24tc; /NASA: 35cr, 44cr; /Peter Ryan: 55tr; /David Weintraub 66t. **Frank Spooner Pictures:** 8bl, 16cr, 17tl, 22tl, 23b, 23cr, 35tl, 42cl, 47crb, 49cl, 56b, 58tl, 59bl, 61tc; /Nigel Hicks 69tr. **Syndication International:** 31cr; /Inst. Geological Science: 32cl, 47tr; /Daily Mirror: 57tr. **Woods Hole Oceanographic Institute/Rod Catanach:** 24tr. **ZEFA:** 9tl, 34tr.

All other images © Dorling Kindersley.
For further information see:
www.dkimages.com